FRISCO
PIGEON
MAMBO

AIVIA
PRESS | PRESS

FRISCO PIGEON MAMBO

C.D. PAYNE

AIVIA Press
www.nicktwisp.com

Sebastopol, California

FRISCO PIGEON MAMBO. Copyright © 2000 by C.D. Payne. All rights reserved.

Manufactured in the United States of America.

10 9 8 7 6 5 4 3 2

Cover illustrations by Joanne Applegate.

Library of Congress Cataloging-in-Publication Data

Payne, C.D. (C. Douglas), 1949-
  Frisco pigeon mambo / C.D. Payne.-- 1st ed.
    p. cm.
  ISBN 1-882647-24-6
  1. Pigeons--Fiction. 2. Birds as laboratory animals--Fiction. 3. San Francisco (Calif.)--Fiction. I. Title.
  PS3566.A9358 F75 2000
  813'.54--dc21

00-009906

To my parents and sisters

Special thanks to my agents Winifred Golden
of Castiglia Literary Agency, La Jolla,
and Jon Klane of Jon Klane Agency, Beverly Hills.

CHAPTER 1

"Heard the latest rumor?" asked Petey, puffing placidly on the Drag-O-Matic. "The word is we're actually pigeons."

"I am *not* a pigeon," stated Honky with conviction, fluttering his wings. "Am I, Robin?"

"Of course you're not," I agreed. "And neither am I. I don't know where Petey gets such preposterous notions."

Petey coughed, expelling a millet seed, then spoke. "Robin, take your beak out of that sherry tube, and answer me this: If we are not pigeons, why do they feed us Hygienic Pigeon Chow?"

My ID band tinkled softly against my leg as I scratched at a nit. "They feed us Hygienic Pigeon Chow as part of a scientific experiment," I said. "We are explorers on the frontier of knowledge."

"Hmmphh," snorted Petey, puffing away. "An experiment designed to prove exactly what?"

"I suppose that humans can thrive on Pigeon Chow," I replied. "I find it quite satisfying, especially served with a nice dry sherry."

"Me too," agreed Honky.

"Besides," I noted, "why would Dr. Milbrene name a pigeon Robin? That would be too absurd."

"Why *did* he name you Robin?" asked Honky.

"I think he was inspired by the russet tinge of my feathers," I explained. "Robin is, I believe, Latin for red."

"And why was I named Honky?" inquired my pal. "Is it because my feathers are pure, stark, unadulterated white?"

"Exactly so," I replied. "Honky is Latin for 'white.' Just as Petey is a common colloquialism for 'grossly corpulent'."

"Your scholarship is as miserable as your puny physique," replied Petey, puffing sedately.

"Petey!" snapped Honky, "don't bogart the Drag-O-Matic!"

"OK, OK. Keep your feathers on." Petey edged his porcine bulk over on the perch. He is a broad, grey-feathered fellow with a prodigious appetite for tobacco, sunflower seeds, and (so he thinks) knowledge.

"What are we smoking today?" I asked, sipping from my sherry tube.

"Chesterbogs," answered Honky, blowing smoke rings at Petey's head.

"Damn, I prefer Kalms," I said. "I wonder what brand Sam Spade smokes?"

Lovely Maryanne, our favorite lab assistant, has been reading to us from *The Maltese Falcon*, a book she's studying in class. She's an English major, which Petey says is a British military officer of middle rank. She certainly looks wonderful in her uniforms. She has downy fine golden feathers, slender nearly nude wings, and an attractively prominent bifid breast.

Maryanne is reading to us to take our minds off Wallace, our cagemate who died recently. What a shock. We woke one morning and there he was down on the soiled litter paper—with his toes in the air, stiff as a cuttle bone. Later, I heard Dr. Milbrene tell Maryanne to dissect his cardiovascular system and centrifuge his liver. I imagine that is some sort of solemn funeral rite. I only wish we'd been invited to the services.

A shady character named Joel Cairo just offered Sam Spade five thousand dollars for a statuette of a black bird, then pulled a gun on him. Fortunately, Mr. Spade wrestled away the pistol and knocked the fellow unconscious. I'd love to pursue an exciting career as a detective, though I'm not entirely clear what such a vocation entails. Modern writers are so lax in defining their terms. What exactly is "five thousand dollars?" And how similar is "apartment 1001 at the Coronet" to a stainless steel laboratory cage? I hope the author intends to explicate these mysteries soon.

I'm feeling a little edgy today. Petey is monopolizing the Drag-O-Matic again. I can't understand why everyone has his own personal sherry tube, but we're forced to make do with just one Drag-O-Matic. Petey theorizes that Dr. Milbrene is trying to induce stress in our lives. But why would he want to do that? The man is like a father to me.

Dr. Eli Milbrene is a world-renowned professor of biology at the University of California at Berkeley. Petey, Honky, and I are elite volunteers assisting him with his research as part of Test Group C. We're obliged to smoke cigarettes, drink sherry, and consume regulated quantities of Hygienic Pigeon Chow. Group B residents, in the next row over, have to do their seed munching and smoking entirely sober. Group A subjects are even more deprived. All they're permitted to do is dine on Hygienic Pigeon Chow and go up on the roof periodically for something called "fresh air." I don't know why they're called the "control group." They have so little control over their own happiness.

Group D members are the real party animals. They smoke, booze it up, and dine on rich delicacies like deep-fried prawns, cocktail wieners, macadamia nuts, barbecued pork ribs, and chocolate cheese cake. Often we can hear them down at their end of the lab whooping it up.

Wallace, before he died, confided he'd heard rumors of a Group E, caged in another room. The same delightful lifestyle as Group D, with the further stimulation of mixed-sex cohabitation. Perhaps it was just wishful thinking on his part. Wallace was always sweet on Julie, a Group A experimenter who lives across the aisle with Darla and Blanche. All nice, plain-feathered girls, if a little controlled, but clearly not in the same league as my dear Maryanne.

Sitting on her lovely finger last night after our reading, while she softly stroked my head, I felt the most exquisite tingle suffuse my body. Pleasant but unnerving. Could this be love?

Honky just dropped a large sunflower seed on Petey's head, freeing up the Drag-O-Matic.

"I'm next in line after Honky!" I announced.

"Go pluck yourselves," grumbled Petey, theatrically daubing sherry on his ruffled noggin.

* * *

Honky says we're smoking Marlrubos today, a brand that often causes me to gaze with a steely glint toward the western horizon. This is not as easy as it sounds—especially when one's eyes are situated on opposite sides of one's head.

We all have our particular talents. I am also able to walk without bobbing my head excessively. Petey can empty an entire sherry tube while remaining upright on his perch. And Honky can decipher the labels on cigarette cartons. He used to read the profoundly obscure inscriptions on lab assistants' T-shirts, but gave it up to appease Petey, who—though illiterate—fancies himself the intellectual of our cage. It's hard for a self-acknowledged egghead to confess he is as perplexed as the rest of us by the phrase "Young Dickheads Total Pillage World Tour."

Dr. Milbrene just made his daily rounds through the lab. "Hello, men," he said, stopping at our cage and making notations on his clipboard. "How are we today? Any signs of a palsied tremor or hacking cough?"

Dr. Milbrene is so solicitous of our welfare. He's a true man of the people, even though he's on everyone's short list for the Nobel Prize. Every time the lab phone rings, I expect it's long-distance from Stockholm. Usually, though, it's Eldon, our flunky day-shift lab assistant, calling in to say he overslept.

I'm smoking heavily today; my nerves are on edge. Last night in Sam Spade's apartment that slimy Joel Cairo got into a fight with nice Brigid O'Shaughnessy. As the quarrel escalated into violence, two police detectives arrived and threatened everyone with arrest! Now Mr. Spade's being followed by a sullen youth with a gun.

Petey says adolescents are the price parents pay for the pleasures of procreation. I must weigh this carefully before making further advances toward Maryanne. Yesterday I sat on her shoulder and nuzzled her silken perfumed ear. Wonderful!

Damn, the butt got stuck in the ejector impeller. Now the Drag-O-Matic's jammed. If slothful Eldon doesn't shuffle by in the next two minutes, someone's going to get his rude anatomy pecked the next time he opens this cage!

"Hi, Robin," called a voice from the Control Group A cage.

"Oh, hi, Darla," I replied distractedly.

"You sound like you're sober today, Robin."

She's right. In my agitated state I'd been neglecting my sherry tube. I took an emergency swig.

"The roof was beautiful this morning," she continued. "A gray haze lifted, and you could see all the way to the Golden Gate."

"Was it open?" I inquired, making an effort to appear interested.

"Was what open?" she asked.

"There's no point talking to him, Darla," sniffed Blanche. "The fellow's drunk. They're all a bunch of cage-bound, inebriated, nicotine-breath rubes."

"The sweetest music on earth," noted Petey: "the prim condemnations of the self-righteous prude."

"Hear, hear," said Honky. "Can I buy you fellows a drink?"

We turned our backs on the ladies and bellied up to our beverage taps. Down the aisle the Group D gang was crunching noisily into a bag of fried pork rinds. I suppose there must be some sort of world out there beyond the walls of this cozy lab, but I think Honky's right. It really is no concern of ours.

* * *

We're in shock! Brigid O'Shaughnessy is missing! Last night she disappeared on the way to Effie Perine's apartment. Poor Mr. Spade: first his partner gets shot, then he falls in love with a client in distress, and now she disappears. And nearly everyone is trying to pin assorted murder raps on him.

After the reading, swept up in the emotions of the moment, I kissed Maryanne. She responded by pressing her soft voluptuous beak against my head. Never have I experienced such tumultuous emotions. It was all I could do to maintain my composure as she moistened a lab towel and daubed her scarlet beak-coloring from my feverish brow.

After lights out, I sat on my perch and thought of my future life together with Maryanne. Of course, we'll have to get a larger cage—one with a shelf for Maryanne's English books and a desk for my detective business. Honky and Petey can live in the cage next door and come over for sherry parties. Hey, I wouldn't be surprised if Dr. Milbrene gave us a transfer to Group D as a wedding present. Those fried pork rinds should taste pretty special shared with the woman I love.

Thank God the lab assistant stocked the Drag-O-Matic with unfiltered Cramels. There's nothing like a jolt of unexpurgated nicotine to clear the head and calm the nerves. Already Eldon, though hampered by a bandaged thumb, has had to reload twice. His grungy T-shirt, Honky informed me privately, reads: "Extra fries or the Nobel Prize. Have it your way."

"Extraordinarily opaque," whispered Honky.

"Virtually unfathomable," I agreed.

"What are you two cooing about?" demanded Petey.

"We were just remarking how attractive the ladies look today," answered Honky diplomatically.

Across the aisle, Darla and Julie smiled. Blanche studied us coldly through the bars of their cage.

"It's degenerates like you," she observed, "who put a permanent crimp in a girl's nest-building instincts."

"Glad to hear it," commented Petey, not withering under her icy glare. "Child-rearing is such a juvenile pastime."

"I'm feeling a bit on edge today," remarked Honky, sipping from his sherry tube.

"So am I," I whispered. "I feel anxious and restless. Very unsettling. It's worse when I gaze longingly upon dear Maryanne."

"She's very attractive," agreed Petey. "Except for her feet."

"I'm highly attracted to bright red feet," said Honky, admiring his own lumpy, carmine toes. "Maryanne has regrettably hideous feet. Did you see her yesterday in those open-toed sandals?"

I did, I must confess. Her feet were shockingly pale and smooth. Hardly a bump or nodule to captivate the eye. Then again, none of us is perfect. One must not dwell on the shortcomings of one's love. I myself am not as tall or broad-shouldered as one might wish. Nor am I as handsome as Zeb (short for Zebulon) of Test Group D, with his dark, shimmering feathers and film star good looks.

"Robin has very attractive feet," commented Darla. "They're wonderfully red and knobby. Very scaly too."

She's right, of course. How nice of her to notice. I only hope Maryanne is as observant.

* * *

Something is wrong, terribly wrong. The odious fat man Caspar Gutman had just given Mr. Spade a drugged drink when *CRASH*, the door to the lab flew open. Dropping her book in surprise, Maryanne leaped up as a half-dozen masked, black-garbed intruders swept into the room.

"Freeze right there!" shouted a burly man, waving what Petey informed me later was an automatic revolver.

"Who are you?" demanded my love, bravely standing her ground.

"ARF!" barked the invaders.

"Oh no!" exclaimed Maryanne. "Not Animal Rights Forever!"

"Yes!" affirmed the man. "We are liberating this lab!"

"You can't!" pleaded my sweetheart. "Six graduate students have their entire academic careers invested in this project!"

The man sneered under his bizarre gauze-like mask, later identified by Petey as a pair of lady's black fishnet pantyhose. "You're breaking my heart. Seize the animal torturer!"

Two women grabbed Maryanne; she struggled to pull away. Grappling fiercely, they fell back against our cage. Enraged, I leaped toward the bars and locked onto featherless flesh.

"AAIIYYYEEE!" shrieked one of the women. "Something's biting me!"

"Birdie, let go!" shouted her fellow thug, wrestling my dearest into a headlock. "We're on your side!"

I bit down harder, tasting a spurt of warm saltiness.

"Help!" screamed the woman. "He's amputating my elbow! Shoot him, Ted!"

"No!" exclaimed Maryanne, suddenly ceasing to struggle. "Robin, let go!"

Exerting all my strength, I squeezed my jaws in one last ferocious bite, then released my grip. The woman sobbed and pulled away, clasping her injured wing.

"Damn, I'm bleeding!"

"Serves you right!" muttered my love, right before a male invader slapped a length of thick tape across her sweet beak. Rudely, the female thug bound Maryanne's silken wings behind her back with the Drag-O-Matic cord.

"OK, cover the cages," commanded Ted, the gun-toting leader. "Let's start moving them out."

"What's, what's happening?" whimpered Honky, cowering in

a heap with Petey under the Pigeon Chow tray.

Before I could reply, a black cover descended over our cage, blotting out the light, as the only home we'd ever known began to swing and pitch violently.

"Earthquake!" shouted Honky, a whirlwind of panicked fluttering in the tumultuous, all-encompassing blackness.

"No, it's not," gasped Petey, rebounding heavily against the bars with every bounce. "They're taking us somewhere."

"This is an outrage!" shouted Zeb from the Group D cage. "We haven't finished our fried pork rinds!"

"I fear the worst," groaned Petey. "We're all going to be viciously slaughtered."

"Robin, where are you?" called a faraway voice that sounded like Darla's. "Robin!"

"Here I am!" I sang, receiving no reply. "Don't be afraid!"

Suddenly, we were enveloped in frigid air. Metal doors slammed shut, a rumbling mechanical sound roared, and we began to move.

"We're being kidnapped!" I shouted.

Yes, I realized with horror, we were being plucked from our loved ones—just as heroic Samuel Spade had been wrenched from his own dearest Brigid.

CHAPTER 2

"I'd kill for a cigarette," muttered Honky.

"I'd peck my grandmother bald for a drink," remarked Petey.

"I'd give up all my earthly goods for one crummy sunflower seed," I swore.

"You don't have any earthly goods," sneered Petey. "And where the hell are the lab assistants? This place looks like it hasn't been cleaned in years."

"Yeah," agreed Honky, anxiously peering around. "When do they turn on the heat? My feet are close to frozen and there's an icy draft blowing up my tail feathers."

We were huddled in the darkness under a grimy metal box inscribed on the side—according to Honky—with the words "U.S. Mail." Moments before, the kidnappers had screeched to a halt, pulled us rudely from our cage, and clipped off our metal leg bands. Abandoning us in the lonely night, they climbed back into their white motorized box and drove off with our friends into the misty blackness.

"Robin, I have this tremendously urgent desire to return home," confessed Honky.

"Of course you do," I replied. "We all do. It's only human."

"Look!" said Petey. "Some liquid is starting to fall from overhead."

"Maybe it's a dry domestic sherry!" I exclaimed.

As one, we rushed out and opened our beaks to the heavens. A disappointingly familiar liquid splashed into my eyes and down my throat.

"Bath water!" spat Petey, incredulous.

"We don't get baths in the middle of the night," protested Honky. "Don't they know the damn schedule?"

Expectorating violently, we scurried back under the sheltering box as the wretched dribbling intensified.

"Help me, guys," cried Honky, "I've got something gross stuck to my toe."

Pecking gingerly, Petey dislodged a pale lump from Honky's left foot.

"What is it?" asked our alarmed companion. "Is it alive?"

"It's a cigarette butt!" I exclaimed.

"You're right, Robin," said Petey. "Too bad someone flattened it."

"But we could still smoke it," said Honky excitedly.

"We could if we had some way to light it," answered Petey. "I don't see any Drag-O-Matics around here."

"Wait a minute," I said, thinking out loud. "Eldon used to light his cigarettes with a match."

"That's it," said Honky. "We need a match!"

"Excuse me, sir," I called to a small bird-like figure, possibly a pigeon, loitering across the way in a doorway. "Excuse me!"

"You talkin' to me?" he grumbled, fluffing his dingy feathers.

"Yes, do you by any chance have a match?"

"Sure, your face and a seagull's backside. Ha-ha-ha."

I exchanged glances with Honky and Petey as the fellow chortled convulsively.

"Uh, sir. I think you misunderstood me," I said. "We need a match to light our cigarette."

"It's urgent," added Honky.

The fellow stopped laughing. "You dudes aren't from around

here are you?"

"No," I replied. "We're from Berkeley."

"Oh, college boys," he sneered, "I might have known."

"I don't think he has any matches," said Petey.

"Sir," I called, "can you tell us where we are?"

"You're in the big town, boys. San Francisco."

"San Francisco!" we exclaimed.

"And how do we get to Berkeley?" asked Honky.

"Cheat," the stranger replied, guffawing anew at his dismal jest.

"The fellow is an imbecile," whispered Petey.

I decided to try one more approach. "Sir, can you tell us where we could obtain some Hygienic Pigeon Chow?"

"Sure. Garden Court of the Palace Hotel. I've always heard the chow there is plenty hygienic."

"Swell," I replied. "Is it within walking distance?"

"I guess so," he said. "Two blocks east, one block north. But it's quicker to fly."

"Oh, we don't fly," I explained. "We're not pigeons."

"You're not, huh? You guys trying to pass as doves? Well let me tell you, bud, a dove ain't nothin' but a pigeon with fancy PR."

"You don't understand," I replied. "We're not birds at all. We're humans."

"Damn!" he muttered, shaking his head. "This town is really going to the cats."

"What's a cat?" asked Honky brightly.

"Oh, Jesus!" the bird exclaimed, flying off into the downpour.

* * *

After a rough night we're all feeling a little queasy. Unable to light the cigarette butt and growing ever more ravenous, we decided to experiment. We ate it. The tobacco was moderately palatable, but we could barely gag down the paper and the fuzzy stuff at the end. At least the fragrant beak-coloring stains reminded me of my dear lost Maryanne.

I trust by now Dr. Milbrene has found and untied my love. I hope the professor is coping with the cataclysmic disruption of his life's work. Somehow we must locate our friends, find our way back, and bring those cruel ARF invaders to justice!

As day dawned, more and more boxes on wheels began rolling by our shelter. Frigid bath water continues to dribble annoyingly from the sky. Crowds of people are walking by, some holding odd little cloth domes on sticks over their heads, and a few, I noted enviously, smoking cigarettes. Why, I wonder, isn't everyone enjoying this delightful pastime? If only there were some way to ask for a neighborly smoke for me and my pals. Or a quick toot from a sherry tube. Odd, we seem to have a much easier time communicating with birds and other lower life forms.

Honky just pulled a rubbery substance off the concrete and is attempting to eat it. From the distinctive aroma, I think it may be that material Eldon used to chew when he was foolishly trying to give up smoking. Odd, he never could masticate it sufficiently to permit swallowing. Honky seems to be having the same trouble. I hope the substance doesn't begin manifesting its other strange quirks.

"Look, Phyllis," said a woman passing by. "That white pigeon down there is blowing a bubble with its gum."

"Don't stop, Wendy," said her companion. "It's probably been trained by professional pickpockets."

* * *

I never realized the world was so full of people. San Francisco is teeming with them, of every shape, size, age, and color. And so rude! They just plow forward and expect us shorter fellows to hop out of their way. And shockingly callous! Heading off to our long-delayed breakfast at the Palace Hotel (Honky had to lie down to rest for some time after finally swallowing his gum), we saw a giant box on wheels roll completely over a grey bird-like animal, possibly a pigeon. The box did not stop, and no one except us paid the slightest attention to the tragedy.

"Maybe the poor bugger just had the wind knocked out of him," said Honky, stunned.

"The guy is flattened to less than five millimeters," replied Petey, studying the pancaked corpse. "He's a goner."

"Petey, quick!" I shouted. "Get out of the way!"

Petey leaped back just in time as another giant box on wheels, filled with people hanging from poles, rumbled by.

"Only walk when the tall people walk," I instructed my friends. "See, the rolling boxes seem to stop for them."

On the way to the hotel we paused in front of a rusty yellow box displaying the morning newspaper.

"Honky, what does it say about the lab raid?" I asked. "Is Maryanne all right?"

Honky looked up and read the banner headline: "Big Cost Overruns Expected for New Fighter Jet."

"Are you sure you got that right?" demanded Petey. "I remember hearing about that story a long time ago on Eldon's boombox."

"That's what it says, guys. No mention of the raid. Looks like we don't rate page one. I'm totally depressed."

"I'm more depressed than you are," announced Petey. "I'm lost in a strange city, I'm wet, I'm cold, I smell bad, I'm crawling with parasites, I haven't slept a wink, my feet hurt, and every nerve cell in my body is incessantly clamoring for a smoke and a drink."

"That's nothing," said Honky. "I've got all those miseries, plus a giant wad of previously chewed gum is congealing my insides."

"Come on, guys," I said, walking on, "let's settle this over breakfast."

* * *

The Palace Hotel, we discovered, was an immense gray stone structure rising imposingly above bustling crowds of damp people.

"I guess this is the place," I said. "I hope they're still serving breakfast."

Resolutely following an elderly man in through a strange revolving door, we ducked behind a miniature tree in a shiny golden pot.

"O-o-oh, it's nice," exclaimed Honky. "Feel this plush litter paper."

"Very posh," agreed Petey. "Which way to the pigeon chow?"

"This way, I think," I said, trying not to be intimidated by the opulent surroundings.

We slithered through a doorway leading to a large room redolent with enticing food aromas. Overhead a vast glass ceiling glowed with exotic, jewel-like colors. Here and there elegantly dressed people, seated at small cloth-draped tables amid a veritable pygmy forest of miniature trees in pots, were feeding themselves with sparkling metal implements. White-coated lab attendants, bearing bottles of liquids—possibly sherry—moved silently from table to table. In a corner four black-garbed performers stroked shiny wooden boxes with thin sticks, producing harmonious waves of soft screeching.

Elegant to be sure, but we only had eyes for the long white-draped table along the near wall. There, laid out in splendid array, was a feast to tempt even the most jaded Group D gourmand. In a flash we were behind the table and reconnoitering the situation.

"I'm going off my Pigeon Chow diet," declared Honky. "For good. I hope Dr. Milbrene won't be upset."

"I think he'll understand given the circumstances," I said.

"But how do we get up there?" asked Petey. "Boy, I wish we could fly."

"If wishes were horses," replied Honky, "beggars would ride."

"Spare me your dimestore homilies," retorted Petey.

"We'll have to tug our way up the tablecloth with our beaks,"

I said. "Let's go, men."

The climb was arduous, unaccustomed as we were to strenuous physical labor, but soon even Petey had heaved his disheveled bulk upon the glistening white surface, laden with shimmering plates piled high with rich delicacies. Not a millet seed in sight. We dove in.

"O-o-ooh, these crispy savory items are delicious," called Honky, crunching into thin brown strips.

"I can recommend this slippery stuff," said Petey, slurping down small black globules.

"You can skip the chilled slimy matter in the iridescent shells," I shuddered. "It's ghastly!" I tasted a slender pale item. Much better. A bit salty but good.

"EEK!" cried a voice.

We looked up from our banquet. An elderly woman with a deceased furry animal draped around her shoulders was pointing a pronged metal implement at us.

"Help!" she screamed. "Pigeons are trampling on the buffet!"

"How revolting!" declared her companion, an elderly male nearly devoid of head feathers. "There's a damn feathered rat standing in the kippered herring."

Attempting to appear inconspicuous, Petey ducked behind a tall mound of fuzzy golden spheres. I leaped out of the herring and splashed breast-deep through a tray of warm yellow sponginess. Honky, too startled to move, stared bug-eyed at the couple and began to gag.

Across the room a door flew open, and an angry lab attendant ran toward us carrying a menacing stick with a bristling, fanned out end.

"Let's get out of here!" I shouted.

Petey dived head-first off the table. Honky continued to gag and heave, finally disgorging onto the woman's plate a large wad of pink chewing gum.

"Oh my god! It's his stomach!" she screamed, dropping to the floor like a stone as the approaching lab attendant waved his stick above his head.

I shoved Honky off the table and jumped after him. We bolted toward the door as Petey puffed after us, pursued by screaming lab attendants, several irate box strokers, and the unconscious woman's rat-loathing companion. Somehow we made it through the revolving door just ahead of the vengeful mob, darting to safety between the legs of startled pedestrians.

We fled down the block, turned the corner, and kept on running until Petey collapsed to the concrete exhausted.

"I can't go another step," he gasped.

"That's OK, Petey," I said. "I think we're safe now."

"Why are people so selfish?" demanded Honky. "We eat so little and they have so much. Why?"

"I don't know why," I replied. "Perhaps we made a mistake. Perhaps they knew we were in Test Group C and weren't supposed to be eating that food."

"Well, they could have been a little more gracious about it," said Petey, getting back his wind. "Feathered rats indeed!"

"I'll tell you one thing," said Honky. "It's enough to make me ashamed to be a member of the human race."

CHAPTER 3

"I think I'm seeing a mirage," said Honky, blinking his eyes.

Squatting dispiritedly under another U.S. Mail box, we were scrutinizing each passerby in hopes of spotting Sam Spade or his secretary Effie Perine. We've agreed that tracking down the resourceful detective is our best hope for locating our friends and getting home. No leonine men with long, bony jaws and yellow-grey horizontal eyes passed by, but at least the irksome bath water dribbling had ceased.

"What illusion are you under the misapprehension you see?" asked Petey.

"I think I see, believe it or not," replied Honky, "a bag. A green, orange, and brown bag."

In our experience that appetizing combination of colors could mean only one thing.

We raced up the block to a large open area where the pavement abruptly stopped and soft green filaments rose lushly out of the ground. On a stone seat a woman, much older and bulkier than Maryanne, was leaning back and sprinkling Hygienic Pigeon Chow on the wide plateau formed by her prominent bosom. An enthusiastic crowd of bird-like animals, possibly pigeons, had alighted on her old, white-specked sweater to dine. Famished, we quickly rapelled up her pant leg and muscled our way up and over the springy surface to the chow.

"Hey, quit your shovin'!" protested a bird.

"Watch it, buddy!" hissed another.

"Now, no fighting," cooed the woman, sprinkling another bountiful wingful all around us. "There's plenty enough for everyone."

As legitimate members of Test Group C, Petey, Honky, and I began to eat greedily. We were entitled!

As we gulped, de-husked, and swallowed, a young man riding by on a small board on low wheels stopped and sat down next to the woman. He had bright green head feathers formed into spikes and a shiny gold ring through his beak.

"Whatcha doin'?" he inquired.

"I am feeding my friends," replied the woman.

"Does that, like, hurt?" he asked.

"Of course, not," she replied. "It's rather pleasant actually. Did it hurt when you got your nose pierced?"

"Nah," he replied. "I was stoned the whole time. My chick did it with a red hot nail."

"That sounds extremely unpleasant," said the woman. "What will you do when you get to be my age and have a hole through your nose?"

"We'll probably all be living on Mars by then," he replied. "The breathing apparatus will be like covering it up."

"Ah," she said. "Then you have given the act some forethought. I'm happy your decision was not made impulsively."

"My chick likes birds," he remarked after a pause. "She had a parakeet, but it like escaped."

"Birds are God's creatures," said our benefactress. "They should not be penned up."

"That's what I told Francesca, but she's still bummed. Did you know there are as many pigeons in this city as people? It's true. I read it in a book."

"That would not surprise me," she replied. "At least not the pigeon statistic. And have you noticed how much more peacefully our pigeon citizens get along than the human population?"

"Yeah, I guess so," he replied. "They seem pretty laid back. I wish I was a bird."

"So do I, young man," said the woman. "So do I."

* * *

Stuffed as we had never been stuffed before (who knows where our next meal will come from?), we strolled heavily through the tree-shaded area. Our keen sense of smell brought us to another stone seat where two men sat smoking cigarettes. Our good fortune held. One man dropped his still-lit butt to the ground. Before he could crush it with his foot, Honky darted forward and seized it in his beak.

"Look, Phil," said the other man. "That albino pigeon is smoking your cigarette."

"So he is, Ed," he replied. "And he seems to be enjoying it too. Oh my, now he's passed it along to his buddy."

"Remember, Phil, when smoking was considered glamorous?"

"Yeah. Movie stars and millionaires with languorous ease suavely lighting up."

"Now who smokes? Lumpy, plaid-shirted tourists from the Midwest and the more sophisticated pigeons of Union Square."

"And us, of course. Oh, have a heart, Ed. That fat one down there wants it bad. Give him your cigarette."

Ed gave his cigarette to Petey, who sucked in deep, satisfying drags. Honky and I continued to share our butt as the men lit up anew.

"I wonder what disease they'll be attributing to it next?" said Phil.

"Probably discover it makes your jolly roger fall off."

"That's when I'll be switching to clove gum."

"With your oral needs, Phil, I'd recommend all-day suckers."

"You're probably right, Ed. Well, there's one study we don't have to worry about. I saw on TV that some animal rights freaks raided a lab at Berkeley. They swiped all the test animals—which as I recall were pigeons."

"Really? I wonder if these are some of them?"

"Nah, they had metal ID bands on their legs. Too bad. It said the university is offering a big reward."

"Look, Phil. Now they're doing a dance for us."

"Quite the pigeon mambo, Ed. I'd say they deserve a reward."

While we tried in vain to convey through elaborate pantomime that our leg bands had been criminally removed, the men lit three fresh cigarettes, presenting one to each of us.

"Well, Phil. It's getting close to show time."

"Time to assure those conventioneers their wine choices are superb."

"Try not to look too suspicious, Phil. I hear 10,000 chiefs of police are in town this week."

"Tell me, waiter," said Phil sternly, "is the sea bass fresh?"

"Certainly, officer," replied Ed. "It passed its urine test yesterday and was fingerprinted only this morning."

"And how is the veal?"

"Innocent on all charges!"

* * *

Night had fallen; after one full day in the big city we were still cold, lost, and homeless. We had been threatened, chased, ignored, trod upon, poked, and kicked. Even the few Good Samaritans who had aided us had referred to us as pigeons—and worse. Was the world really so cruel?

"How come everybody keeps calling us pigeons?" asked Honky, obliged by an unslaked thirst to sip dirty bath water from a puddle in the street.

"Perhaps they know something we don't," ventured Petey.

"It's only blind prejudice," I insisted. "Prejudice and ignorance. Who is the most distinguished intellectual we know?"

"Me?" suggested Petey.

"Hardly," I replied. "Dr. Milbrene merits that distinction. And how were we addressed by that world-renowned scientist?"

"He'd say, 'Hello, men'," replied Honky.

"Exactly," I said. "He addressed us as men. In his expert opinion we were humans. That's good enough for me."

"And me too," said Honky. "Boy, that's a relief. I got enough stress in my life without having a major identity crisis too."

"I smell sherry," announced Petey.

"So do I," said Honky. "It's coming from in there."

A short stroll up from Union Square had brought us to a intriguing establishment outlined in flashing lights and resounding with rhythmic tinklings and peals of laughter. The open door revealed a corridor lined with glass-encased pictures of scowling men with numbers on their chests. In their big, gnarly wings many of them grasped stout wooden sticks.

"A friendly refuge on a chilly evening?" proposed Honky.

"Maybe, maybe not," replied Petey. "Remember what happened at the hotel this morning?"

"We must employ psychology in these situations," I said. "I have a plan."

* * *

"Oh my Lord," said a red-faced man seated on a tall backless chair, "look what the cat just dragged in!"

"No more cream sherries for me, Harry," remarked an elderly woman to a white-shirted man behind a high wooden counter. "I got the DTs. I'm starting to see dancing pigeons."

"Have another," said the man, refilling her glass from a brown bottle. "I'm seeing them too."

"Stay together!" I hissed, rhythmically kicking out my legs and bobbing my head. "And try to move with the beat!"

Everyone in the room turned to stare, including the rumpled, featherless man producing the tinkling sounds at a large wooden box.

"I'm really hitting my stride tonight," he announced, launching into a faster tune. "I'm charming the pigeons right in off the street!"

"You sure are, Joe," replied the elderly woman. "With a little help from Irving Berlin!"

"I don't care what anyone says," declared a large man holding up a beaker overflowing with amber suds. "San Francisco's the greatest city for nightlife on earth. Even the pigeons are trained entertainers."

"Hey, Harry," called the woman, "give me some swizzle sticks. A few of those pretty gold ones."

The man behind the counter gave her three glittering plastic sticks. Holding onto her curiously young-looking head feathers, the woman leaned over and carefully placed a stick in each of our beaks.

"Hey, Joe," she said, "let's hear *The Continental*."

"Sure, Effie," replied Joe.

"It's Effie Perine!" gasped Honky, dropping his stick.

"Boy, has she let herself go," observed Petey, never missing a beat as he prodded Honky to retrieve his swizzle.

"It may not be the same Effie," I whispered, earnestly sashaying to the infectious rhythm and twirling my stick like Petey.

"If only they had little top hats," said Effie. "It would be just like the floor show at the El Morocco back in '43."

"I don't care what anyone says," announced the large, suds-swilling man. "Those were the greatest years anyone will ever know."

"The greatest of all time, Bill," agreed Effie. "I worked all day and danced all night. When did we sleep, Bill? Did we ever sleep?"

"We never slept, Effie. Nobody did. Life was too grand!"

As the tune ended, the people put down their drinks and noisily beat their wings together.

"I don't care what anyone says," said Bill. "That's the most amazing damn thing I ever saw."

"Amazing," affirmed Effie. "And cuter than Shirley Temple's baby pictures."

"Bring those boys up here on the bar," boomed Bill. "And let me buy them a peanut."

Swiftly, we were hoisted up onto the polished wooden counter, damp with puddles of enticing liquids and dotted with slotted white dishes holding lighted cigarettes. We had found the promised land at last!

Ignoring Bill's proffered nut, Petey rushed to grab Effie's Lucky Wham while Honky and I dived beak-first into her drink. Bizarrely sweet, excessively chilled, but unmistakably the real thing: sherry!

"Well, would you look at that," marveled Effie. "Don't that just blast your garters."

"I don't care what anyone says," declared Bill. "I haven't seen carousing like this since Fleet Week fell on Halloween!"

CHAPTER 4

Someone was pounding a large metal spike into my brain, blow by tortuous blow. Then I regained consciousness and discovered it was only a dream—except the excruciating hammer blows went on.

"I think I'm blind," groaned Honky. "All I see is brown."

"Is it a dull medium brown faintly ribbed with raised striations?" gasped Petey.

"Yeah, could be. My eyeballs hurt too much to tell for sure."

"I see it too," replied Petey. "You're not blind."

"Where, where are we?" I croaked.

"Don't ask me," replied Honky. "Last thing I remember, I was chugging sherry as old guys dressed in blue sang *It's a Wonderful World*."

"Those were the police chiefs," said Petey, covering his eyes with his wing.

"A merry bunch," I remarked, struggling to position my head lower than my knees. "Why were those fellows so high spirited?"

"Don't you remember? They won fifty bucks off Harry the bartender," explained Petey.

"How exactly?" I asked. Each syllable I spoke reverberated through my head with its own distinct pang of pain.

"Wagering on our drinking capacities."

"Oh, yeah," I said, the fog beginning to lift. Something vile had died in my mouth. "Harry bet we couldn't drink an entire glass of cream sherry."

"Proved that guy wrong," said Honky. "Too bad our late cagemate Wallace wasn't there. We could have killed the entire bottle."

"I think we did," said Petey. "But I may never mambo again."

"I smell a cigarette," said Honky, sniffing. "Lucky Wham, I think."

"Good morning, my little artistes," said a familiar voice. The brown ceiling suddenly parted, and Effie's frighteningly cragged and puffy face peered down at us, a Lucky Wham dangling from the corner of her ghostly beak. Thin white head feathers had replaced her thick young ones.

"How's my favorite dance company? Hmmm, not so hot, I reckon. You boys look as bad as I feel. Or are you ladies? Oh well, no matter. Come on."

One by one, Effie lifted us from our brown corrugated cell, depositing us gently on a chipped metal table. Nearby a motionless, apparently artificial human head was modeling Effie's tawny young feathers. I coughed and gazed queasily about the smallest, most crowded, least tidy room I had ever seen.

"It's not Pacific Heights, boys," she said, snuffing out her cigarette in a butt-littered dish. "But at least it's not the Tenderloin." She scratched idly at her long, shapeless garment, then extracted three fresh Lucky Whams from a pack on the table, inserted them in her mouth, and lit them with a gold lighter.

"Here, boys. Have a smoke while I rustle up some eats. Try not to drop them. Mr. Patel gets upset when we set our rooms on fire."

"Keep your eyes peeled for Sam Spade!" whispered Honky, puffing away.

"If he's hiding in this room," replied Petey, savoring his smoke, "he'd have to be a midget contortionist."

From a pile of debris, Effie unearthed a round metal object and plugged it into the wall. In seconds it began to hum and glow red.

"Now where did I hide the frying pan?" she asked, looking around. "Oh, right. Think elegant Boston fern." Retrieving a small blackened pan from behind a ratty plant, she placed it on the glowing surface. Next she removed three oval objects from a drawer overflowing with hosiery, struck them smartly against the back of a chair, and emptied their mucilaginous contents into the hot pan, setting off a fierce sizzling.

"Mr. Patel is adamantly opposed to cooking in the rooms," she said, stirring the bubbling mixture with a metal coat hanger. "So I'll have to ask you boys to keep this gourmet experience confidential. Of course, I'd prefer to take all my meals over at the Clift Hotel, but these days we're pinching our pennies. Not that we have many left to pinch after last night's convivialities. That's right, fellas. Flick your ashes in the ashtray. My, you boys are neat smokers. Too bad you can't hold your liquor. By closing time last night you were, pardon the expression, completely shit-faced. Total cat bait, so your kind aunt Effie trundled you home in a gin box. There, I think that's ready. Now, boys, let's put out your smokes."

Effie snubbed out our Lucky Whams, scooped some of the pan mixture onto a stained paper plate, and placed it before us.

"Eat, fellas," she said. "And don't be squeamish, it's technically not cannibalism."

Taking a tentative nibble, I recognized the yellow spongy matter I'd been wading through at brunch yesterday. I nodded to my pals, and we all began to eat with alacrity.

"I'm glad you boys got a chance to meet Bill last night," said our hostess, dining directly from the pan with a white plastic implement. "Isn't he a nice fella? To tell the truth, I'm kind of sweet on the guy. I'm hoping he asks me out. It's hard, though, 'cause men these days are so skittish. Have you noticed that? When they're real young, men are kind of shy around girls. Then they go through a stage where they're all over us. And then they go back to being shy. Like delicate, seventy-five-year-old virgins. So now a gal has to employ a lot of finesse, and sort of sneak up on 'em. They spook easy, don't you know?"

"What *is* that woman talking about?" asked Honky, breakfast decorating his beak and face.

"Sex," replied Petey.

"Oh," said Honky, embarrassed.

* * *

After breakfast, Effie lit fresh Lucky Whams for all and turned a knob on a black box next to the artificial head. A big window in the box lit up, revealed tiny dimensionless people in thin, form-fitting clothing jumping up and down to rhythmic dance sounds.

"Time for our morning exercise," said Effie, sitting in the chair and watching the box. I noticed she was taking drags on her cigarette in time with the beat. We decided to join in.

"O-o-oh, that's cute, boys," she said. "You guys are so talented. But don't overdo it. We smokers are in no condition for strenuous aerobics. Believe it or not, I used to have a body like those gals." She laughed, coughing out a pleasant cloud of blue smoke. "But don't ask me to tell you what *I* did to stay in shape."

After our smoke and exercise, Effie switched off the box and opened the lone window—a tall, narrow one looking out on the drab buildings across the street. "Well, boys, it's been fun, but as you might expect, Mr. Patel is adamantly opposed to pets. And your Aunt Effie has to dress and make herself presentable. Do watch your step on the way out. Now don't be strangers, you hear. Come back anytime."

Our hostess ushered us out the window, shut it behind us, and closed the blinds. What a nice woman I thought, temporarily dazzled by the morning sun. Maybe she is the real Effie Perine after all.

CHAPTER 5

"That woman is trying to murder us!" screamed Honky.

"Such inexplicable blood lust," exclaimed Petey. "I'm surprised she's not peering through the blinds and watching as we plummet six floors to our deaths."

We were stranded on the narrow stone window sill, raw terror wedging us tightly against the dust-streaked glass. Far, far below, across a fearsome void, boxes on wheels rumbled back and forth, occasionally bleating out angry cries.

"Robin, I feel my toes slipping!" shouted Honky.

"Hold on, men!" I said. "Don't look down!"

"This is an execution," said Petey grimly. "She administered the cigarette and last meal. Then came the final march toward the brutal extermination of life. The death warrants have been signed. The gods have sanctioned our fate. We're doomed."

"Oh, for heaven's sake, Petey," I said. "Buck up!"

"I'm getting dizzy, Robin," squealed Honky. "I can't hold on much longer!"

"Good morning, pigeons," piped a thin, high voice. "Enjoying the view? That's Sutter Street down there."

We looked up. Perched on the window top was a small bird-like animal. Predominantly green, he exhibited a riotous palette of lurid yellows, oranges, reds, and purples; resembling, if anything, one of Eldon's more flamboyant tie-dyed shirts.

"Hello, bird," gasped Honky. "Can you fly us down to the ground? Please!"

"Gentlemen, I am a parakeet, not a cargo pelican. After a heavy lunch, it's all I can manage to get myself airborne. Why don't you fly yourselves down?"

"We can't," I explained. "We're not pigeons, we're humans."

"Ah yes, there seems to be quite a lot of that going around now," he said. "Well, they say identity is one percent genetics and ninety-nine percent misapprehension. For a time I myself imagined I was a mental health professional. That fixation proved somewhat transient, thank God."

"Can you help us at all?" I pleaded.

"Well, I could offer one modest suggestion."

"What?" demanded Petey.

"You could jump down to the wide ledge under your window, and follow it around the corner to the fire escape. Then hop down the stairs."

Honky leaned cautiously forward and peered over the edge. "We're saved!"

"Of course," added the bird, "there is one problem with that plan."

"What?" Petey asked suspiciously.

"There's a cat down in the alley prowling around. A big, nasty, scary one."

"What exactly is a cat?" I asked, determined to clear up this issue once and for all.

"A cat, for those who may have dropped recently from a comet, is a sly rogue sent by the devil to waylay the unwary. He lurks in the shadows, poised to pounce on the young, the old, the infirm, and the generally delusional. Cats should be given a wide berth, especially by feathered pedestrians."

"What should we do?" asked Honky.

"I suggest you hop down to the ledge, make yourselves comfortable, and wait until I tell you the cat has departed."

* * *

"My name is Gerigar, first name Bud," said the parakeet, gliding down to join us on the ledge. "Please don't call me Sigmund Hombird."

"Why would we do that?" I asked, introducing my friends and myself.

"Because that's my actual name," he replied, nodding affably through his embarrassment. "I think it's bilious. That's one of the reasons I left."

"Left where?" asked Honky.

"Home, such as it was. I formerly lived at the Fillmore Street Mental Health Center. I was the resident Cheer-U-Up bird, a thankless role let me tell you. What a flock of lachrymose whiners, especially the staff. Ladled up the pessimism with a shovel. I did the best I could though."

"What did you do?" asked Petey, intrigued.

"Oh, cracked jokes. Whistled. Sang songs. Dispensed advice."

"You mean you can actually talk to people?" I asked. "Besides us, I mean."

"Oh, sure. The human lingo is not difficult once you get your tongue properly twisted. Of course, you have to maintain contextual dissonance. People get nervous if you start making too much sense. They like to think they have a monopoly on rational thought. No offense."

"No offense taken," said Honky.

"How do you maintain this, er 'contextual dissonance'?" I asked.

"Well, say I'm sitting in on a session. I'm standing there on my perch, getting a dreary earful, and I happen to say, 'Divorce that lying cheat while you've still got your looks.' The client and therapist look up in surprise. Then, admiring myself in my mirror, I add, 'Nuclear war is bad for budgies.' *Voila,* contextual dissonance. But meanwhile, the client has heard at least one piece of sensible advice."

"That sounds like an interesting job," said Petey. "Why did you leave?"

"The usual reason," replied Mr. Gerigar. "Professional burn-out. That and the crummy eats. Money got tight so they had to cut back somewhere. One morning, pecking through a tray of moldy Mexican birdseed, I told a suicidal client to get a 'grip or get a gun.' That afternoon I flew out the door during a family crisis melee."

"Did you know a girl there named Francesca?" asked Honky.

"Doesn't ring any bells. We had a client named Francis, but she offed herself. Another nice morale booster for the staff! Who's Francesca?"

"Oh, she's a person we heard about who lost her parakeet," I explained. "You haven't run into it, huh?"

"Wish I had," said Mr. Gerigar. "A guy gets pretty lonely out here."

"We're not sure the missing bird is a female," noted Honky.

"That's OK," said Mr. Gerigar. "In this town it doesn't really matter."

CHAPTER 6

We've all got the shakes; we need a drink in the worst way. No immediate prospects for slaking our thirsts, but at least Mr. Gerigar has stayed with us to help. He says we cage escapees should stick together. We're desperate to get home, but he seems actually to enjoy living on his own in this immense, terrifying city. Of course, it's easier for him since he can fly. Sometimes I think I won't be able to fight back the panic for one more second. I just feel like screaming. I can't believe they don't have Drag-O-Matics on every corner in this town. How do people cope?

Besides saving our lives, patrolling for cats, and escorting us to an exotic area called Chinatown for a gourmet lunch of fried wontons (gathered from a remarkable culinary emporium called a "dumpster"), Mr. Gerigar's been supplying us with life-sustaining smokes. He mines the shiny cans outside building entrances, dredging through the fine white sand for still-smoldering butts. Then we puff away madly until the dormant ember revives. He even found an enormous brown cigarette that, tragically, was too heavy for him to dislodge. We stood in anguish on the pavement—our bodies trembling, our heads pounding—as the greatest smoke of our lives slowing turned to ash just out of reach.

"Maybe you fellows should reconsider the concept of flight," remarked Mr. Gerigar, puffing tentatively on a Virginia Gaunts which Petey had resurrected. We were huddled in a sunny doorway around the corner from an immense sign of a naked woman with red bulbs flashing in the center of her featherless breasts. (I must check someday to see if Maryanne is so equipped; such an erotic attraction might compensate for her disappointing feet.)

"I told you, Mr. Gerigar," I said. "We're humans, not people. That's why we have to find Sam Spade and get back to Berkeley."

Over lunch, we had filled in our new friend on the harrowing events of the past few days. He said he had no idea how to get to Berkeley, but could introduce us to a well-connected cardinal if we ever wished to fly down to Stanford.

"People *can't* fly," added Honky. "It's damn inconvenient too. My feet are in ruins. I need some comfy shoes. And maybe a nice warm raincoat."

Mr. Gerigar coughed, gasped for air, and passed his cigarette butt back to Petey. "Those things are dreadful," he said. "I can't believe you suck that filthy poison into your body."

"It's very satisfying once you get the hang of it," I assured him.

"A hat too," continued Honky. "And a scarf. A nice wool one like Effie's."

"Pack along all that baggage, Honky, and you'll never get off the ground," said Mr. Gerigar.

Petey puffed thoughtfully on his cigarette. "Our wings don't seem as atrophied as a typical human's."

"Now, Petey," I said, "don't start in on that again."

"I'm not saying we're pigeons. I'm just saying perhaps some people, a small minority, *are* equipped for flight."

"Not as many as are equipped for homicide," observed Honky.

"Flying is easy!" exclaimed Mr. Gerigar. "It's all a matter of mental outlook."

"Mine is pretty dim at the moment," confessed Petey. "I fully expect each new day to be my last."

"I'm not surprised," noted Mr. Gerigar. "Excessive walking is a powerful depressant. Let me teach you fellows to fly! It'll be fun."

"Sorry, Mr. Gerigar," I said. "I've never seen a person fly. It's impossible. Thanks just the same."

"I think shopping for comfortable shoes would be a more sensible use of our time," replied Honky. "Something foam-padded, with good arch support."

"Well, dammit, I'm willing," said Petey, taking a final, deep drag on his salvaged butt. "Flight school, huh? Where do I sign up?"

* * *

"OK, stretch out your wings like this," said Mr. Gerigar, demonstrating the proper stance.

Petey puffed on an Old Goldplate, and stuck out his disheveled wings.

"Now flap," said the instructor.

Both began to flap; the teacher rising nimbly into the air, the pupil lurching about in an out-of-control stagger.

"How high did I get?" asked Petey.

"About as high as a nit's ankle," replied Honky.

"Spit out that cigarette!" commanded Mr. Gerigar.

"Why?" demanded Petey.

"Because every ounce counts when you're trying to levitate a hippopotamus."

Offended, Petey reluctantly passed his stogie to Honky.

"OK, this time," said Mr. Gerigar, "we're going to face into the wind, flap our wings, and run. When you feel your feet leave the pavement, continue flapping smoothly."

"Flapping smoothly, right," repeated Petey.

They ran down the sidewalk. Flapping his wings smoothly, Mr. Gerigar soared gracefully into the air. Lumbering heavily, Petey huffed five meters and collapsed in a heap.

"I need a drink," he declared. "No sane person should try to fly dead sober."

* * *

"Booster rockets," muttered Mr. Gerigar, scratching his head. "Auxiliary engine power." He whistled loudly, and a flock of tiny bird-like animals flew down from a nearby building.

"Petey," said Mr. Gerigar, "meet the Finch brothers."

"In a pinch, call a finch," chirped the largest of the miniature birds.

Mr. Gerigar positioned three finch volunteers under Petey's chest and four more under the stern. "OK, men. When I give the signal, everyone flap as hard as they can."

"Including me?" asked Petey, doubtfully.

"Especially you," said Mr. Gerigar. "OK, go!"

The finches fluttered, Petey flapped, and, miraculously, daylight began to appear under his feet. He rose several centimeters, wallowing first to the left and then to the right. After several seconds of thrilling flight, all seven booster rockets flamed out, sending the experimental craft careering landward in a cloud of feathers. Amazingly, all parties survived, including the dazed finch at the bottom of the pile.

"Forget a finch," he chirped weakly. "Get a winch."

"Well, I guess I proved that people can fly," grunted Petey, rolling stiffly off another flattened Finch brother. "Now, let's go look for some shoes. And a drink."

"I know just the place," said Mr. Gerigar.

CHAPTER 7

Dodging pedestrians and boxes on wheels, we followed our friend a half-dozen blocks to a tall building that tapered eccentrically to a point far overhead in the clouds. Flying from wire, to pole, to branch, Mr. Gerigar led us around a clump of trees to a concealed pit topped by a grid of metal strips. We gathered beside him on the concrete rim of the pit. A stream of warm air billowed up from its unknown depths.

"OK, Petey," instructed Mr. Gerigar, "walk out on that ventilator grate and flap your wings."

"I'd rather not," he replied, puffing on a soiled Bison & Hackers he had rescued from a gutter.

"Come on, Petey," I said. "Aviation calls. Remember, flying is your destiny."

"You can stick that one in your crop," he retorted. Sighing, Petey passed his cigarette to Honky, and stepped gingerly out on the grate.

"Flap your wings," said Mr. Gerigar. "Let the updraft give you lift."

"I'm getting a lift," mumbled Petey, not flapping. "I'm definitely getting a lift out here." He stood motionless in the warm blast, a quizzical expression, almost a leer contorting his face.

"Petey, what are you doing?" demanded Mr. Gerigar. "Extend your wings and arch your tail feathers!"

Ignoring his flight instructor, Petey tiptoed toward the center of the grate. "Ooh, it's even stronger out here. Fellas, you really ought to give this a try."

I glanced at Honky, who shrugged, put down his cigarette, and stepped out on the grate. I followed.

A rush of humid air enveloped my body; I suddenly felt buoyant and lightheaded. Strange, delicious sensations rippled up from the torrid rustlings below. Pleasurable waves welled up in my body, each sensual quiver tingling with the same exquisite, rosy reverberations as the touch of Maryanne's ruby beak.

"Wow," swooned Honky, "this is something else."

"A curiously satisfying phenomenon," I agreed, edging closer to the center.

"Mystics have long ascribed magical properties to the pyramid," commented Petey. "Close your eyes and feel the power."

"I feel it," I said. "I definitely do."

"Hell, it's better than booze," said Honky. "Mr. Gerigar, get your little green ass out here, guy. This is too fabulous to miss."

"You fellows are disturbed, deeply disturbed," sighed the parakeet, watching us forlornly from the rim. "Cat food on the hoof and proud of it to boot."

* * *

We're all extremely jealous. Honky has procured his shoes. A nice pair of color-coordinated white Oxfords in approximately his size. He's been clopping around pleased as punch, admiring his reflection in a large piece of tin foil. It'll serve him right if he trips and breaks his neck; no one can figure out how to tie the laces.

Honky stumbled upon the discarded footwear while excavating a cheese-laden stratum of ravioli in the course of a somewhat heavy Italian meal in a dumpster in North Beach. Not only was the metal lid ajar, but the aromatic dumpster had been positioned against a gently sloping wall, affording excellent pedestrian access. We even found a bottle containing a few ounces of a mildly stimulating red beverage. Not sherry, alas, but a pleasant complement to the lingering mellowness from those profound "Grate Vibrations." In fact, we only ventured away from our windy pyramid because Mr. Gerigar insisted he was starving.

"My feet are *so* toasty," exclaimed Honky, pecking away at the dried pasta still clinging to his miniature shoes. "I hope you boys won't get chilled."

"We'll manage," I said.

"Shall we dance into the taverns and get loaded?" asked Honky, clumsily attempting a few mambo steps.

"OK, but not Effie's bar," I insisted.

"Get loaded with what?" slurred Mr. Gerigar. Though he continues to condemn tobacco, our friend had found the red beverage quite to his liking.

"The nectar of the gods," replied Petey. "Sherry!"

* * *

We never made it to the bars. As we strolled down the alley toward a street lined with lively night spots, a pair of oddly bald youths swaddled in billowing folds of giant-sized clothing rode by on two-wheeled tubular metal appliances.

"Look, Toby," said one, stopping and pointing, "there's a funky white pigeon ova there wearin' baby shoes."

"Bet his mommy dressed him like that, Casey," said his friend. "Let's go grab 'em."

The hoodlums dropped their vehicles and ran toward us.

"Trouble, fellows!" warned Mr. Gerigar. "Fly!"

Alarmed, Petey and I fled back up the alley, as Honky hobbled after us. Brave Mr. Gerigar did his best to harry the advancing youths.

"Get away from me, bird!" shouted the taller of the two, waving his arms.

"Call a cop! Call a cop!" shrieked Mr. Gerigar, swooping

around their heads.

"Grab that pigeon!" bellowed the other tough, closing in on Honky. "Don't let him get away!"

Desperate, Petey and I backtracked to our terrified pal, pulled him bodily from his shoes, and shoved him through a narrow opening in a brick wall. We followed, quickly withdrawing into the musty darkness under a building as the two toughs crouched down and peered in.

"Ya see 'em, Tob'?"

"Nah, don't see nothin', Case'. Bastard's in there though. Come on out, birdie, we got your little shoes."

"We just want to put 'em on ya. Don't be scared."

"Drop dead, jerks," we heard Mr. Gerigar say, adding for contextual dissonance, "Better mental health begins at home. Flake off, creeps!"

"The bastard's askin' for it, Casey," said a creep. "Let's go get our slingshots and nail the mother."

"Yeah, maybe we can sell his feathers!"

Seconds after the toughs departed, Mr. Gerigar flew in. "Quick. Let's get out of here, fellows. Before they come back."

"What a gyp," wailed Honky. "Ten-thousand chiefs of police in town, and not a cop in sight when you need one."

* * *

Twenty minutes later we received yet another shock. We returned to our susurrus grate to find it occupied by two coarse, rustic men, lounging in breezy dishabille and guzzling from brown-paper wrapped bottles. Parked nearby were two metal rolling carts piled high with grubby bundles.

"Look, Mack, we got company," said one of the men.

"Who is it, Sam?" asked his partner, taking a swig. "Tell them we're not at home."

"It's a bunch of pigeons, Mack. One of them is smoking a cigarette."

Ever vigilant, Petey had sniffed out a discarded Viceboy on our panicked run down the hill.

"Hey, this is a no-smoking section," slurred Sam.

Ignoring the oaf, Petey passed the cigarette to his despondent shoeless pal.

"Mr. Gerigar," I said, "can you ask these rude trespassers to leave?"

"I can try," he replied doubtfully. "Budgies like their privacy. Please leave, intruders. My uncle drives a Buick. Please leave."

"Hey, Sam. I never heard of a pigeon that could talk."

"It ain't a pigeon, Mack. Issa little teensy bird."

"Where?"

"Up in that tree. See, he's kinda shy. Talks good though."

"Talks better than you do, Sam. Maybe he wants a drink. You want a drink, little buddy?"

"Budgies enjoy refreshments. My uncle's in Baltimore on business."

"Pour him a drink, Mack. Pour one for his uncle too."

"But his uncle's in Baltimore, Sam."

"Yeah, but maybe his aunt's hidin' out in the dark there."

Mack removed a shallow pan from a grungy pack and placed it on the concrete rim. Both men tipped in a small splash from their bottles. Petey, Honky, and I rushed it as Mr. Gerigar flew down to join us.

"Wow, what we've got here, Sam, are some real party animals!"

The rosy liquid was cloyingly sweet, but quite potent. We began to relax and edged out on the stimulating grate. Mr. Gerigar remained expectantly beside the emptied pan.

"The only thing I ever had in my life," cried Honky, his feathers fluttering, "were those shoes. And people stole them. Why? Why are people so cruel, Robin?"

"Not everyone's cruel, Honky. These fellows, for example,

they're being quite pleasant."

"Too bad that fat pigeon there smokes, Sam," remarked Mack. "Bet he'd be good eatin' otherwise."

Alarmed, we backed away from our rude companions.

"Yeah, Mack. Nothin' like 'em splayed open and barbecued. We used to have 'em all the time over where I was campin' under highway 280. The babies are even better."

That did it! Something snapped in my mind. I rushed toward a swollen, dirty red ankle and bit down hard. Mack bellowed in pain as Honky and Petey attacked his companion and Mr. Gerigar mounted an aerial assault.

"Killer pigeons!" screamed Sam, scrambling up and lunging for his cart. "Run for your lives!"

Mack limped after his companion, as Mr. Gerigar harried their drunken retreat from above.

"Guess we showed them," said Honky, smoothing his feathers as he bounced up and down on the grate. "Good going, Robin."

"Send in the cats!" I said, my heart still pounding. "We'll show this damn town we can't be pushed around!"

"Cancel that last request," said Mr. Gerigar. "We've had more than enough drama for one night. Oh look, someone forgot his bottle."

No marauding cats showed up to interrupt our party. Good thing for them too. Later, more icy bath water began dribbling out of the sky, so we spent the night inside a newspaper rack. We sent Mr. Gerigar up the coin return slot to jimmy the mechanism, then we all pushed down on the spring-hinged door and hopped in. We were snug and dry, and figured that any cat who wanted to attack us would have to pay fifty cents for the privilege. Mr. Gerigar curled up in a sports section and dropped off immediately, while the rest of us reclined on Dear Abby.

CHAPTER 8

Our third morning as desperate refugees in the big city. Still no sign of Sam Spade or our fellow escapees from the lab. Flight school has resumed on a broad plaza at the foot of four towering, slab-like buildings lined up across a broad street from an immense body of murky bath water glinting green in the vaporous light. At one corner of the plaza a disorderly pile of massive concrete pipes gushed water into a foaming pool. Mr. Gerigar thought it might be an old sewage plant that had been abandoned or bombed. On its mossy walls, more rustic rolling-cart men and women reclined in the pale sunshine.

Honky and I shared a Stalem as Mr. Gerigar prepared the reluctant airman for his latest act of gravity-defying bravado: gliding.

"Petey, you have to glide before you can fly," said Mr. Gerigar. They were poised at the edge of a low concrete wall. "Now, stretch out your wings."

Petey eyed the potentially bruising concrete at the base of the wall and listlessly raised his wings.

"No wonder you can't fly!" exclaimed Mr. Gerigar. "You've got the wingspan of a canary. I never noticed it before. What happened to your feathers?"

"Maryanne clipped them," explained Petey. "She barbered us every other Tuesday."

"I could use a trim right now," I said, feeling a fresh pang of epic longing at the mention of my love. "So could Honky. We're all starting to look a bit shaggy."

"No trimming," insisted the parakeet. "There will be no more trimming! You need those feathers. We must undo the mischief of that damn Delilah. Come on, we're going to find Petey some wings."

* * *

"What is it?" Honky asked. In the shadows behind the gushing sewage plant lay a grisly pile of bloodied feathers and miscellaneous disembowelings.

"What *was* it is a better question," said Petey, shaking his head.

"It was a seagull," said Mr. Gerigar. "I spotted it this morning while scouting cigarettes for Petey."

"What fiend could be responsible for so savage an act of wanton depravity?" I demanded.

"It was the falcon," said Mr. Gerigar.

"The Maltese Falcon!" we piped in unison.

"I don't know about that," replied Mr. Gerigar. "It was the peregrine falcon who lives on the roof of the Mark Hopkins Hotel. I didn't know he had a taste for seagull; he usually dines on pigeon."

I looked around at my pals and coughed. "Well, fortunately, we don't have to worry about that. What does this falcon look like? Is he gleaming gold, encrusted with dazzling precious gems?"

"Not that I noticed," replied Mr. Gerigar. "He's big and terrifying. He's the biggest, fiercest bird I've ever seen. You'll know him when you see him."

"I don't want to see him!" exclaimed Petey.

"Another reason to learn to fly," said Mr. Gerigar, sorting through the feathers. "You fellows are sitting ducks on the ground."

* * *

Once again Petey was poised on the low wall, his stubby wings now augmented with the macabre remnants of a deceased seagull.

"I feel like an idiot," he said.

"You look like Jack the Ripper," commented Honky.

"I hope those feathers hold," said Mr. Gerigar, tucking in some ghoulish loose ends. "OK, Petey, thrust out your wings, leap forward, and feel yourself soaring."

"More like feel yourself sorely," giggled Honky.

"I need a drink," announced Petey.

"We all have our cravings," replied Mr. Gerigar. "But we're suppressing them. What we need right now is for you to show some guts and jump off this wall."

"If the flies are any indication, he's showing more than enough guts already," observed Honky.

"Go for it, Petey!" I called. "You can do it."

My friend raised his wings, closed his eyes, and launched his feathered tonnage into space. Amazingly, he did not fall like a brick, but sailed forward in a neatly controlled descent, landing beak-first more than seven meters in front of the wall.

Honky dropped his cigarette. We stared at each other in stunned bewilderment. We had witnessed a miracle: sedentary, overweight, uncoordinated, intellectually overburdened Petey had flown!

"Where am I?" he asked, rubbing his beak.

"Bravo, Petey!" exclaimed Mr. Gerigar. "That was a tremendous glide. Absolutely first-rate!"

"Hell, it was nothing," said Petey modestly. "Some people just have a natural gift for flight."

On his second glide Petey sailed three meters farther. On his fifth glide he dipped one wing and turned. On his ninth glide he flapped his wings, turned, turned again, and landed *back on the same wall*. That was no glide, that was a flight!

"OK, Mr. Gerigar," said Honky, "you've got another volunteer. Suit me up, guy."

"Me too," I said. "Let's go raid those seagull remains."

* * *

When we returned in our sanguinary flight garb, the plaza wall was crowded with well-dressed people dining from brown paper bags in the warm noontime sun.

"Oh, my God, Tom," said a woman, pointing at Honky. "That seagull's all bloody."

"I don't think it's a seagull," said her companion. "It looks to me like a white pigeon, disguised as a seagull, possibly injured—though I think not—and smoking a cigarette down to the filter."

Honky spat out the stinking butt.

"Well, it's put me right off my shrimp salad," she said, discarding her sandwich. Petey and I dived for it. "More bloody pigeons!" she screamed, leaping away from the wall. "It's a fucking invasion!"

"Don't get hysterical, Barbara," said the man, tearing off a corner of his sandwich for Honky. "It's just Mother Nature's rich diversity."

"Oh, shut up, Tom," said the woman. "You liberals are all alike."

CHAPTER 9

Guess what? I'm flying! Well, technically gliding, but definitely navigating through space with a void under my feet. So is Honky. Turns are still pretty scary, solid obstacles loom before us with terrifying abruptness, and with each landing sadistic gravity smites one's body with Earth's entire planetary mass. Bruising to the flesh, yet exhilarating to the soul. And what a concrete way to achieve emotional grounding.

The transformation in one's consciousness is profound. A few days ago I was a stalwart bi-ped, looking up at the world from a perspective barely loftier than a bug's. My ambitions were pedestrian—to find comfortable, theft-resistant footwear. Now I'm a creature of the sky, soaring through an unseen medium of suddenly tangible space.

When I arch my wings, I can feel a force bodily pulling me heavenward. Petey says this invisible force is the "power of flight" still resident in the seagull remains. Two mysteries: How long does the power live on in the feathers? And why haven't more people discovered this marvelously uplifting phenomenon?

Nothing makes any sense. We neophyte city dwellers can fly. So why aren't the skies of San Francisco abuzz with human aviators—soaring on surplus seagull feathers, smoking cigarettes, and swigging sherry? I admit it, I'm confused. Why is modern urban life so opaque to reason?

* * *

"Dad! Dad!"

A voice interrupted our aeronautical shop talk as we were sharing a low-tar Demerit up in a tree. How thoughtful of nature to provide so many convenient landing roosts for pilot trainees.

"Dad! I've found you at last!" cried a young birdlike animal, possibly a seagull, alighting on a limb beside Honky.

Startled, Honky passed his cigarette to Petey and exhaled smokily. "Do, do I know you?"

"Dad, it's me, Kenny! Don't you recognize me?"

"Oh uh, hi, kid," said Honky, nervously retrieving the butt and taking another deep drag. "What's up?"

"Dad, Mom's been worried sick! We're going on a picnic to Alcatraz and you're supposed to bring the halibut. What's wrong, Dad? How come you're all bloody?"

"Uh, it's halibut blood," said Honky. "I had to use some serious muscle on the dude."

"Run along, Kenny," said Mr. Gerigar. "Your father is busy now."

"Dad, who are these birds? How come these seagulls look a little like—please don't get offended—pigeons?"

"Don't be silly," replied Honky. "They're, uh, your uncles. This is your Uncle Robin and your Uncle Petey. That's Mr. Gerigar; he's not your uncle."

"Nice to meet you, I guess. Dad, what's that thing in your beak?"

"It's a cigarette, Kenny," said Honky. "Now, you'd better do what Mr. Gerigar says and run along."

"But, Dad, what'll I tell Mom?"

"Tell her it was nice while it lasted, but all good things must come to an end. Tell her I wish her the best and I hope she finds someone else more, uh, compatible."

"But, Dad," protested Kenny, "seagulls mate for life!"

"Don't believe all the propaganda you hear," sniffed Honky.

"We mustn't be a slave to biological determinism," agreed Petey. "Take a powder, nephew. This tree is reserved for adults."

"OK, I'm leaving," said Kenny. "But Mom is really going to be steamed."

"She'll get over it," replied Honky. "Have a nice life, son. Watch out for the Mark Hopkins Falcon."

"Yeah, right," said the callow gull, taking wing in disgust toward the distant bay of fetid bath water.

"Maybe we should have told the poor kid his father got eaten," said Honky.

"Well, it's a little late for that," I pointed out.

"Face it, my friend," said Petey. "You're a family man now."

"Hmmm," said Honky, bogarting the smoke. "I wonder what that chick looks like? I never made it with a seagull."

"You've never made it with anybody," Petey pointed out.

"Yeah," sighed Honky. "Don't remind me."

* * *

Flying is lots of work but definitely enjoyable—as satisfying in its own way as grate lounging. Of course, we're all a little afraid of heights—especially Honky—so we haven't dared venture very high. The best part? No more scrounging for smokes. Petey developed a new motivational technique to refine our flying skills and it works like a charm. We just whiz by and grab that attractive, aromatic stogie right out of people's mouths. Rude, I suppose, but that's life in the big city for you. Anyway, the people seem more startled than offended. I think most of them find it an entertaining stunt, rather like our synchronized mamboing.

This afternoon Honky discovered an ingenious way to dispose of the butts. Soaring gracefully off a NO PARKING sign, we dropped our smoking torpedoes down the shirt collars of several familiar two-wheeled shoe rustlers. Toby screamed, clutched at his shirt, and crashed into a parked box on wheels. Casey bellowed, grappled with his smoldering garments, careered out of control, and came to an abrupt halt against a visiting police chief, who struck the youth smartly with a large stick on his shaved skull.

"Bash him again!" shouted Mr. Gerigar from our vantage point atop a nearby pole.

The police chief complied enthusiastically, as did several of his companions in blue.

"Contextural dissonance," I whispered.

"Make love not war," whistled the parakeet. "These are the times that try men's souls!"

CHAPTER 10

There's been a tragic accident. And it's all my fault.

This morning at my insistence we sneaked into an enormous banner-draped building where, according to Honky, some sort of computer exposition was underway. I reasoned we might get lucky and spot Dr. Milbrene, who often spends long hours closeted in his office massaging his computer data, whatever that is. Well, we didn't encounter anything that I'd care to massage—just a lot of buzzing machines, great throngs of people lugging around bulging shiny bags, and no Dr. Milbrene.

Eventually, we wandered into some sort of giant room where a geeky guy with glasses was giving a demonstration. Still no Dr. Milbrene. As we ducked under a table, Petey tripped over a cable, dislodging it from a humming machine. At that moment we heard the audience gasp in surprise. I peeked out to see what was up, and I noticed the geeky guy's face was turning red.

"Gee, that's odd," he said. "This software has been beta-tested by over one million users. It's never done *that* before."

Crack! A tremendous flash sent a flying mass hurtling toward me. I hit the deck. The mass streaked past my head, impacted a wall, and rebounded, knocking Petey off his feet. As the smoke cleared, I realized with a shock that the feathered missile had been Honky. Slowly picking ourselves up, Petey and I gazed in horror at our stricken pal.

"Uhhhhh," moaned Honky. "My foot!"

"Oh my God!" exclaimed Petey.

I couldn't believe my eyes. Where only this morning had wiggled a robust red foot, there was now an alarming void.

* * *

Somehow, with Mr. Gerigar leading the way, we managed to haul our delirious companion through a maze of teeming corridors and out to an open, park-like area across the street. Now we're trying to get a grip on our panic and figure out what to do next.

"What could have happened?" I asked, dazed.

"He must have stepped on some sort of booby-trapped wire," speculated Petey. "Or maybe that computer was seriously overdue for its massage."

"I suppose I'm a goner," groaned Honky, stretched out on the green filaments under a tree.

"Very likely," agreed Petey gloomily. "You won't live long without a leg. Some cat will get you for sure."

"Don't be silly," I said. "We'll look after you, Honky. Are you in great pain?"

"I will be if someone doesn't bring me a cigarette fast."

Seconds later I was back with a Cramel 100, borrowed hastily from a surprised computer fancier.

"Am I still bleeding?" asked Honky, exhaling a cloud of blue smoke.

"You never bled a drop," replied Mr. Gerigar, studying Honky's stump. "The heat of the flash must have cauterized the wound."

Honky gazed up at the heavens and sucked greedily on his cigarette. "You've been great, fellows," he said. "Thanks for the wonderful times."

"Just lie still," I said. "You'll be fine."

"It's my time, fellows," he replied. "I'm seeing a sign."

"What sort of sign?" asked Petey, intrigued. "Do you see a

great white light? I'm told the hallucinogenic pyrotechnics at the end can be quite spectacular."

"No, I see Wallace," replied Honky. "Our old cage buddy."

"But Wallace is dead," I pointed out. "Dear Maryanne centrifuged his liver."

"Of course, he's dead," replied Honky. "That's why I see him. He's come to welcome me home."

"Who's Wallace?" inquired Mr. Gerigar.

"A former Berkeley cagemate of ours," said Petey. "Had the hots for Julie as I recall. Honky, how do you know it's Wallace?"

"Well, for one thing he's smoking," answered our pal, his features now composing themselves into an expression of profound grace. "Hello, Wallace!" he called.

"What's up, seagulls?" came the startling reply. "How did you know my name?"

We looked up in amazement as Wallace himself flew down and landed beside our pal. The ghost puffed on his butt. It was comforting to know that in heaven smoking was permitted.

"Wallace," I said, "does the phrase 'Extra fries or the Nobel Prize' mean anything to you?"

Wallace dropped his cigarette. "Oh, my God! Pluck out my gizzard and call it paté. It's my long-lost buddies!"

* * *

Wallace's improbable story of how he returned from the dead:

"Hey guys, all signs to the contrary, when I was sacked out on the bottom of the cage, I wasn't really expired! I was just sleeping it off. Next thing I knew sweet Maryanne was coming at me with the biggest knife I'd ever seen. And no, Robin, she wasn't just intending to cut some flowers for my funeral. That woman had dismemberment on her mind. So I panicked and flew out the window. All of which came as another big shock to me—this flying business, I mean. I guess I sort of made it up as I went along. Suddenly, I'm six stories above the ground with shorn wings that couldn't support an emaciated gnat. It's a miracle I survived the impact. Then I had to get up and run from Maryanne. The woman came after me! She turned completely homicidal. I was lucky to escape down a sewer grating. Hey, I need a smoke.

"Good old Eldon," continued Wallace, returning with a fresh cigarette and resuming his tale. "As a lab assistant he sucked, but I really owe my life to that dude. After hiding in the sewer pipe and nearly being devoured by a pack of ravenous rats, I decided there was only one thing to do—go home. I mean, the lab was the only home I'd ever known. All I could do was hope that Maryanne had been restrained by then or been arrested or had her grants revoked. So I hid in some bushes until I saw Eldon come out on his lunch break. While he was smoking one of his funny cigarettes, I crawled unnoticed into his backpack. Then, undetected by Eldon, I rode back up to the lab, where I received another terrifying shock. I heard Dr. Milbrene yelling at Maryanne for not centrifuging my liver. He said my escape was imperiling their data. He said if he had to footnote the discrepancy in his papers he was going to mention her by name. That's when she swore she would not rest until I was found, returned to the lab, and dissected. The words made my blood freeze. I realized that home was not a healthy place to be, even if they did provide free eats and plenty of cigarettes and booze. Too terrified to move, my liver numb with fright, I remained in the backpack."

"And you subsequently rode in the pack with Eldon to San Francisco?" asked Mr. Gerigar.

"Eventually," replied Wallace. "With many traumatic stops along the way. We spent hours in one place where the music was so loud I thought my ears would burst."

"Eldon was probably rehearsing with his garage band the Sniveling Idiots," said Petey. "I hear they're dreadful."

"The pits," confirmed Wallace. "Like having red-hot cage bars poked in your ears."

"I'm sure Maryanne did not mean you any harm," I said. "You have to realize you were part of an important scientific study. You were not authorized to leave."

"Well I did," said Wallace. "And I'm glad too. Except I do miss that Drag-O-Matic and sherry tube. I've been sober for weeks."

We all clucked in sympathy.

"Eldon must live in San Francisco," I said, thinking out loud. "If we could find him somehow, we could ride back to the lab in his pack!"

"You could if you were insane," replied Wallace.

"We *must* get back," I insisted. "All of us—especially now that Honky's been injured. I'm sure this mix-up can be explained. Maryanne and Dr. Milbrene would never harm us. They wouldn't, they couldn't."

"Go back if you want, Robin," said Wallace. "But I'm staying here. Phoebe needs me."

"Who's Phoebe?" asked Honky, intrigued.

"Get up off your backside, you one-legged malingerer," replied Wallace, spitting out his butt. "And I'll show you."

* * *

Wallace, believe it or not, is cohabitating with a female. After persuading Honky that even amputees can fly, he took us home to meet his missus. We followed him along the edge of the bathwater bay to a place called the Pierside RV Park. Mounted on a tall pole above a garish electrical sign was a miniature home on wheels, complete with real glass windows, a sundeck above the forward living room, and what Petey identified as a roof-mounted satellite dish.

"Do you really have TV?" asked Honky enviously.

"No," admitted Wallace, circling proudly above his elevated dwelling, "but we hope to someday."

We landed on the little stoop outside the door and followed our friend inside. The interior was cramped, but not uncomfortable. Mr. Gerigar thought the cheery yellow curtains on the windows were a homey touch. And they provided a stabilizing beakhold for Honky, who was learning to teeter about on his left leg.

"Hi, hon," called Wallace, "I've brought some friends over."

"Wally, I'm in no condition to entertain," snapped a female voice from the adjoining room. "You know I'm sitting on eggs. And I think I'm starting to moult."

"Don't fret, babe," said Wallace. "These are my oldest pals. We were at college together in Berkeley."

Curious, we peered through the narrow doorway, then glanced away in embarrassed silence.

Wallace noticed our discomfort. "OK," he said, lowering his voice. "She's a pigeon. What of it?"

"Nothing, Wallace," I said. "She's very . . . attractive."

"A lovely bird," agreed Mr. Gerigar. "Is this your first clutch?"

"Yeah," replied Wallace, obviously in need of a cigarette and a cocktail. "A guy looks around for a good time and then, boom, he's got a house, a mate, and kids on the way."

"It's perfectly natural," declared Mr. Gerigar. "And healthy. We all envy you."

"Yeah, right," said Wallace. "You want to go up on the sundeck? There's a nifty view of the bay up there."

"Sure," I said.

"Nice meeting you," called Honky.

No reply from the feather-lined nesting chamber. We filed out and helped Honky up onto the sundeck. Out on the green bathwater bay an enormous vessel piled high with red boxes steamed by. Below us, large versions of Wallace's home glinted in orderly rows on the wooden pier.

"Boy, I wish you guys would ditch those stinking seagull feathers," said Wallace. "You don't really need them, you know."

"But they possess the power of flight," protested Honky.

"Bullshit," said Wallace. "*You* possess the power of flight. Your feathers are long enough now. Strip, guys, and be what God intended you to be."

"What precisely is that?" asked Petey, reluctantly plucking out his auxiliary flight equipment.

"God, I wish I knew," said Wallace. "But that's not the point. Men, there're four of us now, plus your parakeet pal. That's enough to do the job."

"What job?" I asked. "You mean find Sam Spade?"

"Not exactly, dudes," he snorted.

CHAPTER 11

We were lined up on a utility pole across the street from a store Wallace had spotted on the edge of Chinatown. Not only was the front door kept propped open for anyone to enter, but the front window was glistening with row upon row of tiny glass bottles—all perfectly sized for ease of carrying.

"OK, men," said Wallace, "you all know your jobs. Let's not have any slip-ups. Any time you're ready, Mr. Gerigar."

The parakeet nodded and catapulted off into the night. He flew straight into the store, fluttered around the thin, elderly man behind the counter, alighted on the flashing security camera, and said, "Hey, mister, your fly's down."

Taking advantage of the clerk's temporary preoccupation, the rest of us glided in to grab the goods. Attempting a pinpoint landing on a glass shelf, I misjudged my speed, over-slid my target, and sent bottles flying in all directions. Recovering quickly, I grabbed a bottle, launched into a glide, and collided with Wallace, who ricocheted into Petey, forcing the bulky airman (recently designated by Wallace as "the flying brick") into an emergency landing on the nearest horizontal surface—the surprised clerk's head. The man grabbed a club from under the counter, swung it at Petey, missed, and delivered a stunning blow to his own gray-feathered scalp.

Petey leaped from his collapsing perch, grabbed a bottle from the window, swerved around Wallace and sideswiped Honky, causing our handicapped pal to drop his cargo. Flapping erratically, Petey lurched out the door as Honky spiraled down out of control. Just then another man ran in from the back carrying a large, menacing gun. Mr. Gerigar buzzed his head, shouting "Don't shoot! Don't shoot!"

The man fired, plaster blew out of the ceiling, I dropped my bottle on his head, he fired again, and the front window disintegrated in a spectacular explosion. The man turned his gun toward Honky dazed on the floor, Wallace dived-bombed his face, the gun went off, a gray blur zipped in and hauled Honky out the door, I zoomed after them, Mr. Gerigar passed me like I was flying backwards, the gun went off again, more bottles exploded on the wall beside me. Then I was outside and flying for my life as bullets whizzed around me.

* * *

"I need a drink," said Honky, still dazed.

"Well, keep your feathers on," muttered Petey. "You'll get one as soon as I figure out how to get this damn cap off."

"What's in that bottle anyway?" asked young Kenny, bouncing up and down in the center of the ventilation grate.

"It's sherry," said Petey, pecking at the bottle top. "It's even better than the grate."

"Get that bottle open!" commanded the seagull, basking in the sensual updraft. "Hey, Honky, can I have a puff off your cigarette?"

"Oh, uh, sure," said Honky, passing him the nearly new Mall Pall that Wallace had swiped off a carousing police chief just moments before.

Kenny inhaled, coughed, smiled, and inhaled again. "That's fine, really swell. You guys really know how to party. What did you say you are again?"

"We're people," explained Wallace, pecking feverishly at his bottle cap.

"Yeah, I figured you dudes weren't really seagulls. Good thing you dropped that masquerade. Some guys in my flock might not take that sort of thing so well. Sorry about your leg, Honky."

Floating in the soothing wind, Honky smiled weakly at his rescuer.

"We'd like to thank you, Kenny," I said, "for saving Honky's life."

"Weren't nothin'," he replied, puffing away.

"Don't bogart the smoke, Kenny," said Petey, working on his bottle cap.

"Oh sure. Sorry." Kenny passed the butt to Mr. Gerigar, who shuddered and passed it to me.

"Petey, do try to hurry," said Honky. "My nerves are shot."

"You are fortunate, Honky, that your ass was not shot," replied Petey. "And you are also fortunate that I had the resourcefulness and daring to escape with this bottle."

"I had a bottle too," protested Honky. "Until a big clumsy oaf who can't fly straight made me drop it!"

"Well, the object of your slander just deduced how to open this bottle," retorted Petey, demonstrating for Wallace how to swivel off the cap. "So show some gratitude. And don't spill it!"

Honky took an eager swig, then carefully passed the bottle back to Petey, who drank and passed it to me. Meanwhile, Wallace's life-giving wine was rotating to Mr. Gerigar and Kenny.

"Wow, this stuff is great," said Kenny. "Excuse me a moment, fellows."

Five minutes later the gull returned with a fresh bottle clutched in each foot.

"Kenny!" exclaimed Honky, "how on earth did you get those?"

"The men were busy boarding up the windows," he explained, "so I sneaked in."

"Kenny, you are proving moderately useful," said Petey. "Your presence here is not entirely onerous."

"Thanks, Petey," he replied. "Say, I was wondering, fellas. What do you suppose happened to my dad?"

A sudden pall fell over the party.

* * *

Kenny was taking the bad news like a man. "You're, you're sure it was my dad?" he asked.

"Alas, yes," said Mr. Gerigar consolingly. "I identified the remains myself. There . . . wasn't much."

Kenny sobbed. We all looked delicately away. Several minutes passed in contemplative wine guzzling.

"You know, I've been thinking," said Wallace, lying back in the sensual breeze as far overhead the rising moon gilded the tip of the pyramid an iridescent silver. "I don't think it should come as any surprise to us that people can fly."

"Of course, it shouldn't," I agreed, passing an S&M butt to Honky. "Er, why is that, Wallace?"

"Well, remember how Eldon was always talking about getting high? He obviously could fly."

"Odd, he never demonstrated that talent for us," remarked Petey. "Of course, Eldon was the laziest person I've ever met. And flying is damn hard work."

"You should try it with one leg sometime," remarked Honky.

"The way I figure it, Honky," said Wallace, bogarting the wine, "you just lightened up your load. Hell, I'd saw off a leg too if I had the right equipment."

"Wallace, is it really you?" we heard a voice say. We all turned around in surprise. From the shadows beneath a redwood tree someone approached. It was Julie of Control Group A.

Chapter 12

Love is like a cigarette butt. The ember of passion can burn for a long time untended. Sometimes it flickers out through neglect, or gets stepped on, or burns down to the filter and begins to stink. Other times, a propitious draft will reignite the flame. Such was the case with Julie and Wallace. Neither imagined they would ever see the other again: one parted (apparently) by death, the other separated by an irrational fear of liver centrifugation. Yet, there they were last night, face to face in the moonlight, eyes aglow with rekindled ardor, sweet words of endearment being cooed without apparent restraint. But what of poor Phoebe, molting alone on her eggs back in the trailer? True, she was only a pigeon, yet even a pigeon, it could be argued, deserves some consideration. I trust Wallace will grapple with this moral dilemma soon.

Of the Group A gals, Darla is by far the best flyer. On her own initiative she persuaded Julie and a doubting Blanche to undertake flight experiments. Now she can launch herself from a standing start and fly nearly straight up for hundreds of meters. Looking out for her friends, she located several choice dumpsters, saved Blanche's life by bravely driving away what Mr. Gerigar speculates was a cat, and found them all a snug little home far above the treacherous streets. Julie took us there last night for a gala reunion.

Darla greeted us warmly and bustled about helping make Honky comfortable. Even Blanche seemed almost happy to see us despite the liquor on our breaths. They reside in a metal box attached to an immense panel that rises vertically from the top of a building near Union Square. A motor in the box operates some complicated-looking gears, belts, cams, and shafts. A bit noisy and not something you'd want to snag your tail feathers in, but the heat from the rumbling motor nicely drives away the chill. The ladies have set up housekeeping on a spacious platform above a large, oily lever that slowly rotates back and forth.

"Very pleasant and nicely catproof," said Petey, gazing about. "All this machinery puts one in mind of the Drag-O-Matic. Most homey."

"Rather more dirty and smelly than I'd care for," sniffed Blanche.

"Very resourceful of you to find this place, Darla," I said.

She smiled. "Well, Robin, I was hoping it might help attract the notice of you fellows."

"How's that?" I asked.

"Didn't you see the front?" she asked.

"No, Darla," said Julie, snuggling next to Wallace. "I brought them up the back way."

"Then come along, Robin," she said, brushing her wing against mine. "You must see our beckoning message."

Wallace, Petey, and Mr. Gerigar came too. We flew behind Darla to the front of the panel, ablaze with light from an array of lamps along the top.

"My God!" said Wallace, stunned. "It's the biggest cigarette in the world!"

On the panel the colossal head of a steely-eyed man in a house-sized hat gazed out across the city. His gloved, motorized hand moved the giant cigarette to his enormous lips, then the tip of the cigarette glowed fiery red, the hand moved back, and a big cloud of white smoke puffed from the man's mouth.

"What does the lettering say?" I asked, awed by the splendor of the arc-lit vision.

"According to Julie," replied Darla, "it says, 'I'm hopin' to be ropin' a Marlrubo'."

The mouth puffed again. Petey, Wallace, and I flew into the inviting cloud, inhaled greedily, then nearly plunged out of control to the rooftop below in a fit of coughing.

"I can see why he's hopin' to be ropin' a Marlrubo," observed Mr. Gerigar. "Right now it smells like he's smokin' his rope. And chokin'."

* * *

We spent the night with the gals. Ladies on one side of the platform (Blanche insisted), men on the other side. No drinking or smoking (Blanche again). To no avail Petey pointed out the extreme hypocrisy of the latter prohibition. Too large to fit through the narrow doorway, Kenny excused himself and went home to deliver the bad news to his mom.

The motor droned, the lever creaked, the smoke chamber regularly expelled its unsatisfying vapor. Far below the busy city grew quiet. Sometime before morning Julie returned alone. I felt a body next to mine and recognized Darla's pleasant scent. I slumbered on, happy to be reunited with our friends and more certain than ever that soon we would be returning to our rightful homes in the lab. I dreamed of brave Sam Spade, searching like me for his lost love. Somewhere out there in the gray, fog-feathered city was Brigid O'Shaughnessy and perhaps my own dear Maryanne.

* * *

After a refreshing night, Darla led us on a breakfast excursion to a favorite dumpster in an alley behind a large building Julie identified as Macy's.

"Oh, so you're a reader too," said Honky, hopping clumsily about the disorderly remains of deliciously stale club sandwiches.

"A little," replied Julie. "Oh, here's the morning paper."

Imagine our shock when she and Honky read the bold black headline in unison: "Killer Pigeons Raid Chinatown Liquor Store."

"How can they call us killers?" demanded Petey. "No one was killed!"

"Well, it says here the liquor store clerk received a mild concussion in the assault," noted Julie, still reading.

"Self-administered as I recall," I pointed out.

"And why are they calling us pigeons?" demanded Honky. "I'm no pigeon!"

"The reporter probably was drunk and got his facts wrong," I explained. "I expect the later editions will be carrying an embarrassed retraction. I wonder if Wallace has heard about this?"

"That reminds me," said Julie, "I hope your friend Wallace is having a nice breakfast. Where, where do you suppose he is?"

I exchanged discreet glances with my men. "I'm sure he's . . . not far," I said.

"Follow the buzzing flies," added Petey, quickly changing the subject. "They usually find the choicest morsels."

When we had eaten our fill, I thanked the ladies for their hospitality and asked them to excuse us for a while.

"I suppose you're slinking off to get drunk and smoke those horrible cigarettes," sneered Blanche.

"Most perceptive, as usual," replied Petey, belching.

"Nothing of the kind," I said. "We intend to track down the famous detective Sam Spade."

"Do be careful, Robin," said Darla. "We don't want to lose you again."

"Don't worry," I replied, surprised and touched by her tender expressions of concern.

*　*　*

I peered in through the grimy window. Five meters away Effie was puffing on a Lucky Wham and watching two-dimensional exercisers cavort inside the black box.

"I can't believe I actually flew up this high," said Honky, gazing nervously over the edge. "Man, these heights are terrifying."

"Don't look down," I advised. "Hey, I bet Wallace wishes he had that TV."

"She doesn't seem to be in any hurry to get to the office," observed Petey.

"Probably hasn't bloodied her wings enough yet this morning," replied Honky.

"Your Mr. Spade must be extremely flexible in his secretarial requirements," observed Mr. Gerigar. "Or else she's exploiting some deep-seated mother complex of his."

Four hours later: Effie has styled her removable head feathers, rubbed a hot metal implement over several dresses, laundered an odd undergarment Petey identified as a brassiere, smoked eight Lucky Whams, and flipped through two magazines. Now she's watching the black box again.

"Hey, Robin," said Honky, warming his stump in the sun, "how can you tail someone if they never leave their apartment?"

"I don't know, Honky. I'm new at this detective business. We'll just have to be patient."

Two hours later: More magazines, more box watching, six more Lucky Whams. Honky got a headache from boredom and is now stretched out on the ledge with his head under his wing. Mr. Gerigar has been psychoanalyzing Petey and has come to the preliminary conclusion that our pal is "a large aggregation of quivering neuroses." I could have told him that.

Ninety minutes later: The window suddenly slid open and Effie peered out. The suspect blew our cover!

"Hiya, fellas," she said. "Long time no see. Hey, who's your decorative budgie buddy?"

"Don't mess with me, Argentina," hissed Mr. Gerigar.

"Uh-oh!" she exclaimed. "One of us has had a little accident.

This could be disastrous for your dancing career, *mon cheri*. Good thing you came to your Aunt Effie."

The suspect turned away from the window to rummage through a cluttered drawer in her untidy bureau.

"She may be going for a gun," warned Petey.

Effie returned with a small glittering object clutched in her withered, spotted wingtips.

"I think this should do nicely," she said, catching Honky by surprise and slipping the object on his stump.

"Hey, fellas, I can walk!" he exclaimed, strolling about the window sill on his glittering peg.

"Very nice," said Effie. "Very classy too. It's the top off a Cross fountain pen that a gentlemen friend gave me in 1954. Nice, but I'd been expecting a ring. I misplaced the pen and the fella years ago. Real 14-karat gold. Good thing for you your Aunt Effie never throws anything out. Say, how about Lucky Whams for all?"

I'm not sure Mr. Spade would approve, but we stayed for smokes with the suspect and sampled a refreshing beverage called gin. Quite nice. "A direct jolt to the cerebral cortex" is how Petey described the fiery liquid.

* * *

There's been a major break in the case! Flying woozily back to the billboard, Honky spotted something on a side street and immediately circled down for a closer look. According to him, the faded red letters on an old green sign above a dusty shop window spelled out, "Sam Spade's Mystery Book Shop." Eureka!

"I didn't know Mr. Spade owned a book shop," panted Petey, landing heavily beside me on a thin wire strung between poles.

"In today's economy it's smart to diversify," said Mr. Gerigar, hovering in the air and showing no signs of fatigue.

"OK, men," I said, catching my breath. "Let's go investigate it."

We entered the store as a startled elderly man exited. We

trooped past stacks of dusty boxes, turned down a narrow aisle lined with towering, book-jammed shelves, and warily approached a counter illuminated by a grimy tube lamp. Under the flickering, buzzing lamp sat a small, delicate-looking man, smoking a sinuous cigarette that appeared to be carved from polished wood.

"Uh-oh," I whispered, "Joel Cairo in the flesh!"

"On the shelf behind him!" hissed Petey.

I looked up. The statuette of a majestic black bird! The Malt—

"Cat!" shouted Mr. Gerigar. "Cat!"

Blind, desperate panic. Even Petey managed to get airborne as we rocketed wildly up and down the aisles, scattering cobwebs and customers.

"Killer Pigeons!" screamed one middle-aged man, fleeing toward the exit. "They're attacking all over the city!"

"Where's the cat? Where's the cat?" cried Honky.

"Killer Pigeons?" said Cairo, calming removing the wooden cigarette from his treacherous beak. "Hasn't that been done before?"

"Where's the cat? Where's the cat?" bellowed Petey, crash-landing on the loftiest shelf.

"On the counter! On the counter!" shouted Mr. Gerigar, swooping past.

I looked down from the top of the swaying tube lamp. On a pile of books to the right of Cairo's thin wing lay a formless ball of orange fur that appeared to be asleep. Cairo tapped it on its shoulder.

"Wake up, Pinkerton," he said. "It's time you earned your keep. We're being invaded by killer pigeons."

The cat stretched out a frightening orange paw, opened his eyes, spotted Mr. Gerigar, and was instantly alert. His fierce jaws chattered as he scanned the ceiling, then his amber eyes locked onto me. In the same instant, he dematerialized from the counter in a spray of papers and now loomed directly in front of me on the top shelf of a nearby bookcase. Crouching, he inched toward me as I felt my muscles go rigid under his mesmerizing gaze. I smelled something foul. Cat breath. The world fell away. Time stopped. The entrancing eyes didn't blink. Nothing registered. Only numb terror.

A streak of green flew between us, breaking the spell. The beast pounced. But not at me. I saw something green fluttering between two orange paws.

CRASH!

"My window!" screamed Joel Cairo.

All heads turned. A large fish (my guess a halibut) flopped athletically amid the glass-littered books in the front window.

"Ommphh!" grunted the cat, as a speeding grey mass knocked him and his victim off the shelf. Down they fell, the cat righting himself in mid-air and landing lightly on four paws. Instantly, he sprang up on his hind legs to snare the tumbling parakeet, who was deftly snagged by his tail feathers by a diving seagull. Kenny soared upward, the cat leaped—and missed.

"Let's go, men!" I called. "Out the window!"

*   *   *

"A death wish," muttered the parakeet, smoothing his disheveled feathers. "Is that what you've got, Robin? A pathological death wish!"

"Now just lie still, Mr. Gerigar," said Darla, soothingly.

We were back among our friends in their cozy billboard home.

Despite his strained shoulder and a pinched tailfeather nerve, Mr. Gerigar did not lie still. "Or were you engaged in some sort of up-close field study of the hunting techniques of the domestic feline? Is that what you were doing, Robin?"

"I'm sorry, Mr. Gerigar," I replied. "I guess I froze up. I never imagined cats could be so, so intimidating."

"One almost got me once," admitted Wallace. "Back when I first came to Frisco."

"Oh, Wallace," said Julie, "what happened?"

"I was having a snack on the sidewalk. Pretty late at night. Some tourist lost a gourmet four-course dinner. I think he'd been washing it down with too-much champagne. Quite a feast. Well, all of a sudden I got this awful feeling of dread. Nothing you could put a wing on, but I decided to bail out. I took off about a half-second ahead of this enormous pouncing cat. He'd been sneaking up on me. A ferocious grey one."

"Oh, that's terrible," said Julie, shuddering.

"You got to keep your eyes open, babe," he said, snuggling against her.

We heard a flapping of wings outside. Kenny poked his head through the narrow opening. "It's the pits," he said. "Some creep made off with my fish. I think maybe it was a cop. The place is crawling with them. Damn, that was the biggest halibut I ever caught."

"Sorry, Kenny," I said. "Thanks for rescuing us again."

"I owe you one, Kenny," added Mr. Gerigar. "My services are at your disposal. What will it be—Jungian analysis? Dream work? Some intensive Gestalt therapy?"

"Uh, I'll let you know," Kenny replied.

"Move your ass, seagull," we heard a coarse voice say.

Kenny withdrew his head and Phoebe walked in.

"Who's the moult case?" asked Blanche.

Phoebe glared at her, then turned to Wallace. "In case you're interested, you bastard," said his mate, "your kids just pecked through their shells."

CHAPTER 13

We made the papers again today. On his way back from book-store surveillance duty, Kenny swiped the early edition of the *Chronicle* from a passenger on one of those red wooden cars that rattle up and down the hills on metal tracks. We spread out the main news section on a wind-sheltered corner of the gravel roof below our billboard home—where, by the way, the ladies now remain in silent reproachful indignation. Personally, I fail to see why *all* of the males should be blamed for the transgressions of one.

Honky puffed on a Pallormint and studied imposing black type that graphically thundered: "Killer Pigeons Raid Landmark Book-store." Below it another headline, less strident in its typographi-cal sensationalism, added: "Shocked Merchant Mystified by Un-provoked Attack."

"Unprovoked, my foot," I said. "As if the cad hadn't brazenly assaulted Miss O'Shaughnessy. That's all the provocation any gentleman needs. What else does it say?"

Honky read on, "Uh, it says the attack by the birds came as a complete surprise to bookstore owner Fred J. Dolan, 48, of 120 Ellis Street."

"An obvious pseudonym for Joel Cairo," I pointed out. "Go on, Honky."

"Uh, Dolan estimates his premises sustained damages in excess of $3,500, not counting anticipated vet bills for his injured cat's sprained ankle."

"My heart bleeds for him," said Petey. "Any mention of Sam Spade?"

"Not that I can see," said Honky, tunneling under to an inside page. "Hey, here's a picture of Dr. Milbrene!"

We tugged the pages over with our beaks, uncovering our pal, and eagerly gathered around the smudged reproduction of the distinguished scientist.

"Watch it, Honky," said Petey. "You're dropping ashes on Dr. Milbrene."

"The man looks obviously stressed," observed Mr. Gerigar.

"As well he should be considering his ordeal," I said. "What does it say, Honky?"

"It says he's being sued, Robin. For $950,000. By the parents of two San Francisco youths injured when escaped laboratory pigeons allegedly dropped lighted cigarettes on them."

"We're not pigeons," I insisted. "What does Dr. Milbrene say?"

"Uh, reached at his UC laboratory, renowned biologist Dr. Eli Milbrene denied responsibility for the attack and all recent depredations by the so-called Killer Pigeons. Said Dr. Milbrene, quote: 'Due to their powerful homing instincts, all of our test animals returned to the laboratory within 24 hours of their release. All are present and accounted for'."

We looked at each other in stunned disbelief.

"Robin, what does this mean?" asked Honky.

"It means, I regret to say, that dastardly impostors may have taken our place in Test Group C!"

* * *

"It looks something like a gigantic cigarette, tipped up on its end," I remarked, trying to catch my breath.

Darla frowned. "I suppose you could say that, Robin. Would you like to fly on?"

"No, it's OK. Let's rest here a moment," I gasped, bending over to catch my wind. Darla turned and studied the view from our perch atop the roof of a lofty tower that rose in cigarette-like cylindricality above pale buildings clinging precariously to the sides of a steep cliff. Below us the city stretched in all directions to the shores of the bath-water bay, glistening blue in the afternoon sunlight. I had never been this high.

"Isn't it beautiful?" she asked, apparently not winded by our strenuous flight.

"What?" I inquired, praying I didn't get a beakbleed from the dangerous elevation.

"The view."

"Oh. Yes, well, I suppose. Say, Darla, didn't you find that flight rather tiring?"

"Not at all, Robin. Look, you can see all the way across the bay to Ber—... I mean, to the other side."

"Yes, it's a stupendous distance," I agreed, starting to get my breath back. "Excuse me for a moment."

I flew down to an open observation platform and snatched a cigarette from a tourist who was just lighting up.

"Look, Darla," I said, returning to her side. "I scored a Kalms, my favorite brand. Care for a smoke?"

"No, thank you, Robin. You know, I think your lung capacity might improve if you were to smoke less."

"I have tremendous lung capacity," I coughed. "Like Sam Spade. He's widely admired for his virile smoking."

"Uh-huh," sighed Darla. "I think I've heard quite enough about your Mr. Spade."

"We're going to find him, Darla. We have to."

"Yes, Robin, so you say."

I took in the view as I puffed on my menthol Kalms. "Darla, see that immense spindly structure extending out there across the bath water? What do you suppose it is?"

"Why, Robin, that's the Golden Gate Bridge. Isn't it magnificent?"

"It's big all right. Hey, didn't you once say you could see the Golden Gate from the roof of the lab? That must mean you can see the lab from the Golden Gate!"

"Uh, no, Robin, I never said that. You must have misunderstood me."

"Damn. I wonder which direction Berkeley is from here?"

"It's hard to say, Robin. Shall we go? There's another place I want to show you. I found it a few days ago with Julie."

"Er, how's she doing?"

"She's devastated, of course. I got her to eat a few maggots this morning."

"Oh, she'll get over it," I said.

"I hope so, Robin. Love can be . . . a burden."

"I know what you mean," I said, thinking of my beloved Maryanne. I only hope she isn't presently lavishing her affections on some impostor in my cage.

* * *

"Isn't this pretty?" commented Darla, alighting on a concrete column beside a low wall inlaid with colorful patterns. "It's so quiet and peaceful here."

"Yes, it's very pleasant," I panted, landing heavily beside her. Another taxing flight at dizzying altitudes had brought us to a verdant area thick with fat round trees. Along the oddly decorated wall were a row of wooden benches, entirely empty of smokers at their leisure, I was sorry to see. No Pigeon Chow ladies either. "What is this place, Darla?"

"It's a park, Robin. The George Sterling Glade. He was a famous poet."

"Never heard of him."

"The metal plaque mounted on this column contains some lines from a poem he wrote about San Francisco. According to Julie, it goes:

Tho the dark be cold and blind
Yet her sea fog's touch is kind.
And her mightier caress
Is joy and pain thereof!
And great is thy tenderness
O cool, gray city of love!"

"Tenderness, huh?" I said. "Well I haven't noticed much of that."

"And you're not likely to either," said a voice.

We turned in surprise. In a nearby tree sat a small bird, extravagantly colored like Mr. Gerigar, but with coral rather than green shades predominating.

"You're a parakeet!" Darla exclaimed.

"Uncommon discernment for a pigeon," commented the bird.

"We're not pigeons," I replied. "We're people."

"And more than a little pretentious," said the bird, "That's certainly a human quality. He killed himself, you know."

"Who?" asked Darla.

"George Sterling. All the great poets kill themselves."

"It must be a difficult occupation," I said, thankful I had opted for detective work.

"Difficult and tragic," agreed the bird, "assuming you have any talent at all."

"Do you by any chance know a woman named Francesca?" I asked. "Her boyfriend has a hole in his beak."

The bird gave a start. "I am *not* going back to Francesca! I'd rather plunge into the bay and be eaten by a mollusk."

"It's wonderful being free," agreed Darla.

"Few aspects of existence qualify as wonderful," said the bird. "Life is degrees of dreariness relieved fitfully by acute miseries. Name's Sunny, short for Sunshine."

We introduced ourselves and, at the bird's invitation, flew over to its tree.

"Forgive me for asking, Sunny," said Darla, "but are you a male or a female parakeet?"

"An excellent question," it replied. "I only wish I knew the answer."

"You don't know what sex you are!" I exclaimed.

"Alas no," it admitted. "I was frightfully young when I left the pet store. Hardly more than an eggling. I barely remember my parents. And Francesca, who named me, was completely clueless in that area—as she is on all matters of consequence."

"That's awful," I said. "Tell me, do you feel at all inclined toward nest-building?"

"Not really. All that bustling about and then what do you have? A pile of sticks."

Darla pondered this. "Well then," she said, "do you desire to smoke tobacco, imbibe intoxicating beverages, and cheat on your loving mate?"

"Not so far," Sunny admitted. "Although it might make a pleasant change. Of course, I don't have a loving mate at the moment, being in a state of sexual crisis."

Darla and I exchanged glances. "A case for Mr. Gerigar?" she ventured.

"I think so," I replied. "Sunny, you must come back with us. We know an expert who may be able to help you."

"An expert," said the lugubrious bird, "is someone who ornaments his ignorance with garlands of recondite nomenclature. But do let us make haste."

* * *

Kenny reports that neither his missing halibut nor a person matching the description of Sam Spade has been seen in the vicinity of the bookstore. Most perplexing. We decided to cope with this new disappointment by getting extremely blotto. We sent the busy seagull out on another daring daylight liquor-store holdup, while we raided nearby pedestrians for smokes.

"I can't believe you folks socialize with seagulls," remarked Sunny. "They are seen at all the garbage dumps in town, you know."

"That seagull saved my life," said Honky, puffing on a Chesterbogs. "And Mr. Gerigar's too."

The two parakeets eyed each other skeptically. To everyone's surprise, Mr. Gerigar was not able to inform our new guest of its sex. He explained that Sunny was only the second parakeet he'd ever met (himself being the first), and therefore he was hardly an expert on the species. He has agreed, however, to take the matter under consultation. We are hoping for a quick resolution.

"Hey, who said you could smoke and drink in here?" demanded Blanche, returning with Julie from a dumpster run.

"Blanche, we must be hospitable to our guests," said Darla. "Though I don't see how their choice of refreshments will be at all helpful to Mr. Gerigar's convalescence."

"I knew this billboard would turn into a den of drunken carousing," grumbled Blanche.

To everyone's surprise Julie decided to sample the sherry, though she declined to smoke. Blanche was shocked. "Julie, why are you drinking that vile poison?" she demanded.

"For the usual reasons," she replied. "To deaden the pain mostly."

"But it's Mr. Gerigar who's in pain," Blanche pointed out.

"Well then, I'm helping him," said Julie, downing a not inconsequential swig.

"Of course, now that I think of it," observed Sunny, taking to the sherry like a seagull takes to halibut, "pigeons are often seen at garbage dumps too."

I recall very little about what happened after that. Darla informs me that I passed out with a lit cigarette in my beak and nearly burned the billboard down. I think she's exaggerating. If I didn't feel so wretched, I'd wake up Petey and ask him if he knows how half my breast feathers came to be singed off. Darla tells me

I look like something the cat dragged in. In my present condition I almost wish Pinkerton himself had finished the job.

* * *

More dreary bath water raining down. Sunny and Mr. Gerigar went up early to his office: a small metal box riveted to an upper quadrant of the main machinery housing. Accessible only to parakeets, it provides a private setting for uninhibited personal revelations.

We sent Kenny out for the morning paper, which became so weightily waterlogged in the downpour, he arrived with only a soggy fragment of the front page. Nor, despite repeated attempts, have we had any better success with cigarettes. The damn bath water keeps snuffing them out. My wings are shaking and I can't focus my eyes. My mouth feels like it's sprouting interior feathers. Petey and poor Honky appeared to be in similarly agitated states. We were so incapacitated, Julie had to read the newspaper for us.

"There's another inflammatory headline," she said, studying the damp page.

"What now?" groaned Honky.

She read: "Killer Pigeons Mug Tot; Liquor Raids Alarm Merchants."

"I don't recall mugging any tots," said Petey indignantly. "What does it say?"

Julie read the first paragraph: "Attacks by the so-called Killer Pigeons escalated yesterday as a trio of marauding birds descended on Estuval Garcia, age 3-1/2, of 1609 Valencia Street, and robbed him of a bag of fried pork rinds. The child was shaken, but uninjured."

"We don't steal food from little kids," said Honky. "Too bad too. It sounds like they don't put up much of a fight."

"If I had to guess," said Petey, "I'd say it was the work of the boys from Test Group D."

"It couldn't be," I pointed out. "According to Dr. Milbrene, all the test subjects have returned to the lab."

"Maybe he's lying," suggested Darla.

We all looked at her in shocked surprise.

"Well, people do lie," she insisted.

"Yes, they do," agreed Blanche. "That miserable cad Wallace for example."

Julie pondered the moving billboard machinery as everyone's gaze shifted sympathetically toward her.

"If Test Group D is still in the city," said Darla, "we should try to find them."

"Test Group D is *not* in the city," I replied. "And the person we must locate is Sam Spade."

Darla sighed. "Well, you won't find your Mr. Spade by sitting around and drinking all day."

"She's right, men," I said, somewhat offended. "Let's go."

"But it's pouring outside," complained Petey.

"But I can't get my nice gold peg wet," protested Honky. "It might rust!"

"You're right," I said. "Perhaps this is something I must do by myself."

CHAPTER 14

On my way, I swiped a cigarette from one of a group of well-dressed smokers huddled together out of the cascading bath water in the covered entry court of a tall building. By now desperate for a smoke, I boldly shared their shelter—loitering near them on a potted tree as I puffed madly away on the delicious (and nicely dry) Truel.

"Boy, look at that pigeon work that cigarette," said a tall man. "I'm surprised he's not getting sick."

If the truth be told, I was starting to feel a little lightheaded. I spat out the butt, flew woozily down to the pavement, and wandered out into the drenching bath water, where I soon encountered a squat grey bird, possibly a pigeon.

"Excuse me, sir," I said, "can you direct me to the Mark Hopkins Hotel?"

"Up the street," said the dripping bird, eyeing me suspiciously. "Top of Nob Hill. Why do you want to know?"

"I'm looking for someone," I replied, remembering to answer evasively as all smart detectives do.

"Well, I'd stay away from there, bub, if I were you," said the bird. "There's a giant pigeon-devouring falcon living up there."

"Oh, I'm not a pigeon," I smiled. "I'm a person."

"I'll bet you like fried pork rinds."

"Why, yes, I'm sure I must. How did you know?" I asked.

"Just a wild guess," said the bird.

* * *

I found the falcon near the top of the hotel on a ledge under a sheltering parapet. I darted through a curtain of icy bath water streaming over the edge and landed near the imposing bird. Startled, he turned his magnificent head—all beak and exotic cheekbones—in my direction, his fierce black eyes blinking sedately as he studied me with interest.

"Oh good," he exclaimed in a deep, resonant voice. "My lunch is being delivered today. I hate to go out in weather like this."

"I know what you mean," I said, stamping my feet and shaking my feathers. "You'd think some bright graduate student would invent a way to put a stop to all this bath water nonsense. I presume, sir, that you are the Mark Hopkins falcon."

"I am," he said, chuckling. "I am indeed. And you, sir, impress me as a pigeon who likes to talk."

"Oh, I'm not a pigeon," I explained, "I'm a person. My name is Robin."

The falcon chuckled again. "I like a meal who likes to talk, Robin. Yes, indeed I do. Name's Norris."

"Glad to meet you, Norris."

"The pleasure's all mine, I assure you."

Except for his unsettling allusions to dining, the falcon seemed much more agreeable than I had been anticipating. "Tell me, Norris, are you as strong as you look?"

"Why yes, Robin, it will all be over quickly."

"I suppose, Norris, you must have a tremendous wingspan."

"I do, Robin. So you can empathize with my caloric needs."

"My guess is, Norris, you could carry a great deal more than, say, your average seagull, for example."

"Infinitely more, Robin. In fact I've been known to dine on

the occasional seagull."

"Yes, I know. You recently dined on the father of a seagull friend of mine."

"Be assured, Robin, I enjoyed him thoroughly. Why this reckless curiosity about my lifting capacity?"

"Norris, have you ever heard of the Maltese Falcon?"

"Why no," he said, clearly intrigued. "Does she live around here?"

"No, but I know where it, er, she lives."

"Take me there, Robin!" the bird implored. "I won't eat you if you do. You have no idea how hard it is to get any falcon companionship these days."

"Of course I will, Norris. That's what I'm here for."

"Robin, you are a most remarkable pigeon. Most remarkable."

"Thank you, Norris. But I'm a person, not a pigeon."

Norris peered at me intently. "Well, you certainly look like a pigeon, Robin. A ratty, half-bald pigeon with curiously red feathers. But we mustn't judge by appearances. Funny, I've never eaten a person, although the thought has often crossed my mind."

* * *

"Norris, the Maltese Falcon is inside that building."

Wisps of steam rose from my outsized companion as cold bath water continued to dribble from the sky. We were perched on a pole across the street from Joel Cairo's deceptively named bookstore. A large wooden panel had been affixed crudely across the broken front window.

"Inside you say, Robin? What's she doing *inside* a building?"

"She's being held prisoner, Norris."

"That's awful, Robin. I shall certainly eat the person responsible for this outrage. How do we get inside?"

"Well, Norris, I was thinking you could pick up that loose brick down there and hurl it against the glass door."

"An excellent plan, Robin."

"One thing though, Norris, there may be a cat inside."

"A cat you say," he said, hesitating. "How big is it?"

"Well, he's pretty big. And plenty fierce. His name is Pinkerton."

"I shall eat Pinkerton too. I always wanted to eat a cat. I'll share him with Maltese. Might be a good ice-breaker, you know."

"I'm not sure we'll have much time for dining, Norris. We have to make a fast getaway."

"Oh all right, Robin. I can always pick up a quick cat later."

As I had hoped the brick proved just as efficacious in shattering glass as Kenny's purloined halibut. Joel Cairo rose from his stool with a cry as I soared triumphantly in through the gaping hole. Behind me swooped Norris, his colossal wings seeming to overwhelm the dim confines of the narrow store.

"Holy shit!" squealed Cairo, ducking behind the counter. Alarm flung open Pinkerton's liverish eyes, terror energized his muscles, and he bolted off the counter as papers and books scattered in all directions.

"I'm going to eat you, cat," taunted Norris. "Robin, where's my darling Maltese?"

"Straight ahead!" I shouted. "On the shelf."

"I see her, Robin. Oh no! She's not moving!"

"Don't worry, Norris. They've, uh, wrapped her up. You'll have to carry her."

"Excuse me, miss," said Norris, delicately gripping the statuette in his huge talons. He launched off the shelf and plummeted toward the floor, thudding the heavy statuette against the skull of the cowering Joel Cairo, who slumped moaning to the linoleum. His cat was nowhere to be seen.

"My God, Robin, have I've killed her?"

"I don't think so, Norris."

"We've got to get her out of this metal suit, Robin."

"Uh, there's not enough time, Norris. People will be coming. You'll have to carry her as is."

Breathing heavily, Norris exchanged anxious looks with me, then pushed tentatively against the statuette with his beak. Cairo moaned. Norris turned and bit him viciously in the thigh. I pecked him sharply on his pasty neck.

"Robin, I'll have to lighten my load."

The falcon stepped back and smoothly disgorged the contents of his stomach—several half-digested birds, possibly pigeons—on Joel Cairo's polished brown loafers. When he had finished, Norris belched and wiped his beak on Cairo's brown tweed jacket. "I hope I haven't offended you, Robin."

"No, it looks quite appetizing, especially the slimy red morsels. Can you carry Maltese now?"

"I'll give it a try, Robin. Though I fear I won't be much use on dates if I get a hernia in the process."

Norris gripped the black statuette, flapped his great wings, lurched, strained, cursed, flapped some more, and fluttered down the aisle and out the broken door with his precious cargo. Still no sign of the cowardly cat. I followed behind as Norris and his new love rose laboriously into the dripping grey sky.

"Splendid, Norris!" I called. "You're doing wonderfully."

"God!" gasped the struggling falcon through clenched beak, "what a fellow has to do to get a date in this town!"

* * *

"Robin," said Darla, "may I have a private word with you?"

"Yes, Robin, I think we'd all like to speak with you privately," added Petey.

"Of course," I replied. "Norris, why don't you put Maltese down there under the crossbeam of the billboard? She'll be safely out of the rain there."

"OK, Robin," he replied. "But shouldn't we try to get her out of this damn metal suit? What if she starts to rust?"

"In a minute, Norris. My friends wish to speak with me."

I followed them into our billboard domicile.

"Robin, why have you brought that falcon here?" demanded Darla.

"He's drunk," charged Blanche. "Drunk and insane!"

"No, I'm not," I replied calmly. "Norris has given me his word that he won't eat any of you. He's very nice actually. He helped me break into Joel Cairo's shop and obtain the Maltese Falcon."

"And what's with this sudden compulsion to collect art?" demanded Petey.

"Let me explain," I replied. "We're looking for Sam Spade, right?"

"Right," said Petey.

"OK, so what is Sam Spade looking for?" I asked.

"That's easy," said Honky, "the beautiful and mysterious Brigid O'Shaughnessy."

"Uh, correct." I admitted. "But he's also hunting for the Maltese Falcon. And now that rare and valuable statuette is in our possession. Therefore, instead of *us* trying to find Mr. Spade, *he'll* be looking for us. And with that master detective on our trail, I'm sure we'll be meeting up with him soon."

"Brilliant," said Petey. "Absolutely brilliant."

"Very ingenious, Robin," agreed Darla. "But I'm somewhat confused on one point. Wasn't the statuette on display in a public store? Why didn't your Mr. Spade locate it there?"

"Oh, detectives don't have time to read," I explained. "They lead much too glamorous lives for that."

"What about Kenny?" asked Honky. "He'll go ballistic if he sees that falcon."

"We've got to persuade him to forgive and forget," I replied. "Norris assures me he's prepared to apologize to the lad. Where is Kenny?"

"Taking some egg foo yoong to his mom," said Honky. "She always gets cravings for Chinese food when it rains. Mr. Gerigar and Sunny went along for the ride."

We were interrupted by the sounds of a desperate struggle outside. We rushed to the box opening. The women screamed; Blanche and Julie collapsed in a dead faint.

Norris looked up from the feathery carcass he was dining on. "Hi, folks," he said. "Boy, I was feeling peckish after that work-out. Want some?"

The falcon held out his lunch. It was our late cagemate Wallace.

CHAPTER 15

After the remains had been disposed of (somberly laid to rest in a nearby dumpster), Darla called a meeting in our billboard bunker.

"We are all saddened by this tragedy," she said, "but there are practical issues that must be settled without delay."

"I can see only one course of action," said Sunny. "Robin must do the honorable thing and marry Phoebe."

Darla gasped. "I, I don't think that will be necessary, Sunny. We can all help provide for Phoebe and her chicks. No one proposes to abandon them."

"Robin brought the falcon here," insisted the parakeet. "He's responsible for Wallace getting eaten. He has to marry Phoebe."

"That's ridiculous," said Honky. "Robin can't marry Phoebe. She's a pigeon. Anyway Wallace was only partially eaten. Norris stopped when we told him who it was."

"Sunny's right," I said. "It's my fault Wallace died. I must do the proper thing. I must abandon all my hopes and dreams, and marry Phoebe and live in a non-smoking trailer with two growing chicks that require constant nourishment."

"What a bother," said Blanche. "All this killing and eating and marrying business. Life was simpler in a cage."

"I don't regret it," said Julie softly. "I loved Wallace and now he's dead, but I'll forever cherish the few days we had together."

"She's right," said Darla. "We can't live with our emotions locked away in a cage."

"Emotions exist to provide alibis for inexcusable behavior," said Sunny. "Robin must marry Phoebe and the sooner the better."

"Why don't you marry her, little bird," suggested Honky.

Sunny shuddered. "I couldn't possibly. Mr. Gerigar says I am a very difficult case. Besides, she's a pigeon. Birds of my station do not mate with pigeons."

* * *

"Who's there?" asked the falcon.

"It's me. Robin."

"Hi, Robin. Sorry again about that misunderstanding with your pal. I've decided I'm never going to eat another pigeon—or seagull for that matter. I've apologized to your young friend Kenny. He was very understanding considering the circumstances. From now on, it's only cats for me."

"I appreciate your dietary sacrifices, Norris. But one thing—Wallace wasn't a pigeon, he was a person."

"That's odd. He tasted very much like pigeon, except for his cinderish lungs, rubbery liver, and overall smokey tang. I fear your pal was not in the best of health."

"Don't be silly, Norris. We're all in the prime of life. And how's Maltese?"

Norris edged closer to his metallic inamorata, wedged against the steel billboard beam. "I think she's warming up to me, Robin. I just wish we could get her out of this rigid cocoon."

"I'm sure she's fine, Norris. It's probably helping keep her warm."

"It *is* a nippy night. Say, that chatty parakeet tells me you're getting hitched."

"I might be. Darla and Blanche have gone to discuss matters with Wallace's widow."

"Marriage, huh? That's a big step."

"I know." I thought of Maryanne somewhere out there in that vast expanse of twinkling lights. Would she be devastated if I renounced our love to wed another?

"Do you think Maltese might marry me someday?"

"I don't know, Norris. I wouldn't get your hopes up."

"Why?" he asked indignantly. "What's wrong with me?"

"Nothing, Norris. You're a magnificent bird. It's just that, well . . . Maltese may not be interested in marriage."

"I know. She's not much of a communicator. Still, she's quite attractive in a reserved sort of way. I'd like to thank you, Robin, for bringing us together. It means a lot to me."

"Oh, it was nothing, Norris. Do you mean to say there are no other falcons in the city?"

"None that I've come across, Robin. I can't understand it either. With this city's bountiful pigeon supply, you'd think it'd be swarming with attractive, well-fed falcons."

"OK, Mr. Norris," called Kenny, flying down to join us. "Let's go."

"Where are you two off to?" I asked.

"We're going on a sherry run," replied Kenny. "I'm grabbing the small bottles and Mr. Norris is going for the big ones."

"Well, be careful," I said. "And how about bringing back a bag of fried pork rinds? I hear they're quite tasty."

"You got it, Robin."

* * *

We had a wonderful wake for Wallace, at least the parts that I recall. The wine flowed like bath water. Great quantities of crispy pork rind were crunched through. And late in the evening a few tipsy revelers were brave enough to sample some freshly caught cat. Not bad if you don't mind picking out the furry bits.

Petey has mastered the butane lighter Kenny swiped and is able to light cigarettes at will from the carton of Carletombs provided by Norris. What a relief not to have to raid pedestrians down on the street whenever one craves a smoke—especially since the extensive newspaper coverage has all but eliminated the element of surprise.

I was happy to see that the theft of the Maltese Falcon was major front-page news in this morning's *Chronicle*. I expect Mr. Spade is already following up on this hot new lead, assuming he reads the paper. I only hope he was not out on a bender last night like us and skipped the morning news because of a splitting headache.

I should note *my* throbbing head did not prevent me from paying close attention as Honky read the sensational accounts. Joel Cairo, I'm happy to report, is in the hospital in serious but stable condition with multiple injuries. I was sorry to hear that Dr. Milbrene has been slapped with several more burdensome lawsuits. Alarmed that the liquor store raids have escalated to involve larger birds, the mayor is convening an emergency meeting of the Board of Supervisors, whatever that is. I cannot believe this hullabaloo could escape the attention of Mr. Spade, however preoccupied he may be with Brigid's disquieting absence.

* * *

After breakfast Norris and Kenny wrenched Phoebe's mobile home from its wharfside pole, carried it back here (with the occupants inside), and deposited it on top of the billboard machinery box. We are all to take turns fetching food for little Wallace Junior and baby Ina, while Phoebe decides which of us is to be her chosen second husband. Already Petey and Honky are cheating by trying to appear even less like marriage material than usual. I just had to upbraid Honky for exaggerating his limp, which he denied doing.

Perhaps owing to grief, Wallace's widow is in the midst of the worst moult I've ever seen—the bird is practically naked. I'm trying to be pleasant to Phoebe, but I wish she wouldn't cut Julie dead like that. It's not Julie's fault they both loved the same fellow. Anyway, Julie is a person and she saw him first.

We've been stuffing food down the gaping mouths of Phoebe's pigeon babies like there's no tomorrow, yet still they chirp for more. Pink, squalling, and remarkably ugly, they bristle with damp, half-formed feathers. Not at all like the placid, tidy infant Mrs. Milbrene sometimes brought to the lab.

* * *

While I was keeping a sharp lookout on the roof for Sam Spade, Mr. Gerigar strolled out on a rest break from his afternoon session with Sunny.

"How's the patient?" I asked.

"A most interesting case, Robin. A most interesting case."

"Petey's taking bets on which sex Sunny turns out to be."

"Yes, I'd heard that."

"Come to any tentative conclusions?" I asked.

"These things take time, Robin. A hasty determination could be extremely traumatic if proven ultimately in error. I fear the therapist and patient are both a little at sea on the issues of parakeet sex and mating."

"It's a bit of a mystery for me too," I confided. "Mating, I mean. I had intended to bring the matter up with Wallace. He had some experience in that area, at least with pigeons."

"Yes, he could have been a valuable resource. We do have Sunny's candid descriptions of Francesca's hectic lovelife, but I'm not sure how much is applicable to parakeets—or to ordinary humans for that matter."

"Kenny and Norris aren't much help either."

"No. Your falcon seems to have formed an obsessive attachment to a lump of painted metal. Of course, large birds are not known for their intellectual depths."

"He's lonely, Mr. Gerigar. It's hard to have a romantic life when you're a falcon."

"Yes, looking about the city's bird population, I'd have to conclude that pigeons were the most successful breeders."

"Sometimes, Mr. Gerigar, I almost wish I was a pigeon. Is that cause for concern?"

"Not necessarily, Robin. It could be a very healthy sign. A most positive sign."

* * *

Julie has shocked us all.

Feeling unwell after dinner, she went inside to take a rest, felt a sharp twitch, and laid an egg. Darla and Blanche had to scramble to improvise a nest from old "Killer Pigeon" news clippings before the egg caught a chill. Now Julie's sitting on it in a state of bewildered happiness. Thus, as Petey points out, Wallace continues to burden us with his posthumous progeny.

I'm no expert, but that egg of Julie's seems dauntingly large. Passing such an object must require a sizeable aperture in one's anatomy. I only hope Julie's internal organs are well tethered. One bad sneeze and it seems like she could eject a kidney or two.

More unsettling news. Darla has imposed an indoor smoking ban for the duration of Julie's expectancy. So this evening all the men (plus Sunny) rendezvoused at the great pyramid for some vital strategic planning. Before leaving, I loaded up Norris with the butane lighter, a pack of Carletombs, and the leftover sherry. Along the way Kenny stopped to pick up a halibut (for him) and a fresh bag of fried pork rinds.

"Hey, this is all right," exclaimed Norris, floating his great bulk on the warmly sensual mechanical wind. "I'll have to bring Maltese here. I'm sure she'd love it."

Sunny snickered from underneath a large pork rind it was eating.

"Did I say something amusing?" inquired the falcon.

"These, these pork rinds are certainly delicious," I interjected hastily. "I'm glad I don't have an addictive personality. I could get hooked on them for sure."

The reckless parakeet snickered again. "Love is not only blind," commented Sunny, "it's actively delusional."

"What's that supposed to mean?" boomed Norris.

Kenny looked up warily from his halibut dismemberment. Honky and Petey stopped puffing on their cigarettes and edged away toward the other side of the grate. I glanced entreatingly toward Mr. Gerigar, who shrugged his shoulders in dismay.

"Norris, Sunny's just a little on edge, that's all," I said. "It's feeling anxious because I'm about to divulge what sex it is."

Sunny peered out from beneath the half-eaten chip. "You are! Well don't keep me in suspense, Robin. What the hell am I?"

"I'd be happy to inform you, Sunny," I said. "But first you must promise me you'll show a little discretion in certain controversial areas."

"Oh, all right. I'll shut up about that. Ignorance is not only bliss, it can be a genuinely rewarding lifestyle. Just tell me, Rob. Am I a guy?"

"No, Sunny," I said. "You're a gal."

"Is that right, Mr. Gerigar?" she demanded.

"I would have to agree with that conclusion, although how Robin came to it, I do not know."

"Wow, I'm a woman!" exclaimed Sunny. "I can lay eggs. I can have children. I can torment vulnerable men. Speaking of which, Mr. Gerigar, do you have a date for this evening?"

"I suppose I do now," he replied glumly.

"Damn," said Honky. "I owe Petey six cigarettes."

"I knew Sunny was a female," replied Petey. "No guy in his right mind would have said what she was about to say."

"That was my reasoning exactly," I replied.

"Hey, I've got an idea," said Norris. "Why don't I go pick up Maltese and we can make it a double date?"

"Oh, I don't think so, Norrie honey," said Sunny.

"Why not?"

"Francesca and I have a strict rule," explained the parakeet, "nothing heavy on the first date."

CHAPTER 16

We had a surprise visitor this morning before breakfast. A trapdoor in the gravel roof sprang open, and out bustled the Pigeon Chow Lady, carrying a large plastic shopping bag and looking worried.

"Flee my darling birds!" she shouted. "You must flee this very morn! The city has made a dreadful decision. Our protests have fallen on deaf ears. You are to be trapped and euthanized!"

"Hey, Petey," said Honky sleepily, "what's euthanized mean?"

"Euthanized, euthanized," repeated Petey. "Yes, I'm familiar with that word. Alas, its meaning temporarily eludes me."

"I've been observing your movements," our benefactress continued, removing a fresh package of Hygienic Pigeon Chow from her bag and pouring a generous helping into a metal tin. "I think the police have been watching you too. O-o-oh, there's the peregrine falcon. How glorious—such a noble bird! I think it's marvelous that you've all become friends. I know you're comfortable here, but it's not safe. I hope you can understand what I'm saying. Here's some nice breakfast for you, but after you've eaten you really must leave. No time to waste! I'll be going now because I know some of you may be shy. Stay well, my darlings! Come to me if you need help. I'm in the Square most every day. Good-bye! Good-bye!"

Waving and blowing kisses, she clambered back down the steep stairs and pulled the trapdoor closed.

"Pigeon Chow anyone?" I called.

"Oh, I suppose so," said Petey. "But what I'd really like is some crispy bacon. Or maybe a succulent cat spleen."

All the seed-eaters (except Julie, nest-bound on her egg) gathered at the tin and began to peck at the hygienic meal.

"Wherever shall we go?" asked Darla. "I hate to leave this commodious home."

"We'll find someplace nicer," said Blanche. "Something with less dirt and not so much greasy machinery."

"We're not going anywhere," I declared.

"Oh, but, Robin, we must," protested Darla. "You heard what the woman said. They're coming to trap us."

"We have to stay here," I insisted. "At least until Sam Spade finds us."

"Darla's right," said Honky. "It's too dangerous. Mr. Spade will just have to find us in our new location."

"I agree that relocating is the wisest course," said Mr. Gerigar.

"Of course we must move, Bud honey," said Sunny, busily dehusking a seed. "Moving replaces the tedium of the familiar with the unfolding humdrum of the novel. Anyway, I don't intend to spend my first full day as a ripe young female dodging traps and ducking policemen. Gee, I hope I don't develop any pigeon-like characteristics from eating this stuff."

"It could only be an improvement," commented Phoebe.

Dirty looks were exchanged.

"But how will we move Julie and her egg?" I protested.

"Well, there's an unused room in the trailer," said Darla. "Julie can move in with Phoebe."

"No way," snapped Phoebe. "I'm not sharing my roof with that slut."

"It will only be for the move, Phoebe dear," said Darla. "Just to transport you all safely. I hope, Norris, you're feeling strong this morning."

"Tremendously strong," the falcon replied. "And perhaps a change of scene will help bring Maltese out of her shell."

"If that doesn't work, Norrie sweetie," said Sunny, "you can always try a 90-ton hydraulic press. Oh, I know the perfect spot to move to! You'll all love it. It's South o' the Slot where the true Bohemians live!"

* * *

Sunny's choice for our new home was surprisingly sensible and most appropriate. She led us "south of Market" to a district of low, plain buildings clearly constructed for utilitarian purposes. At the corner of one such building rose a tall concrete tower, upon which an immense sign flashed a message of cordial hospitality across the city. As hundreds of multi-colored bulbs illuminated in turn, one saw a familiar-looking brown bottle tip slowly forward; then an amber liquid flowed from its spout into a round glass. Above and below this animated image more bulbs illuminated in sequence to spell out, as if being written letter-by-letter in yellow light, "Enjoy the Golden Rush, Drink Gold Rush Sherry."

Perhaps to keep out stray pigeons, all openings in the painted sheet-metal sign were obstructed by weavings of stout wire. These Norris quickly plucked out with his mighty talons. Into one of the larger openings he and Kenny pushed the trailer aft first, positioning it safely out of the weather, while still affording an excellent view of the city's skyline to its feuding occupants. As Maltese was too large to fit in any of the openings, she was laboriously lodged against a support strut on top of the sign.

The narrow interior of the sign was a maze of dark metal catacombs, lined with wires and nicely warmed by heat radiating from the bulb sockets. Here and there, small devices—identified by Petey as electrical relays—clicked away like lazy crickets as they operated the lights.

"I don't know about all these wires," said Honky, limping nervously along a passageway.

"Oh, I think they're safe enough," said Petey. "Just don't gnaw on them."

"I wasn't planning to!" replied Honky.

"It's so spacious," exclaimed Darla. "We can have a nursery for Julie and food storage rooms and a place for you boys to smoke, and Sunny and Mr. Gerigar can have their own private apartment, and so can Phoebe and . . . and whomever she chooses to be with."

I coughed. "It appears fairly well defensible too," I said. "I just hope Mr. Spade can find his way up here. He'd need a tremendously long ladder."

"Oh, I wouldn't worry about that, Robin," said Darla. "I'm sure your Mr. Spade can fly."

"Right," I conceded. "He probably can, come to think of it."

* * *

To our disappointment an extensive search of the vicinity failed to turn up any evidence of sherry manufacturing, bottling, or dispensing. Surveying the building's window-lined central courtyard, we saw only oddly dressed people daubing oily colors onto flat cloth panels or manipulating viscous earth into lumpy brown shapes. No one appeared to be drinking sherry either, although a few, I was relieved to see, were smoking avidly.

"Must be those Bohemians that Sunny was talking about," commented Honky, coming in for a lopsided, good-leg-first landing beside me on a sunny ledge.

"A rough-looking bunch," said Petey, fluttering down in his usual falling-meteorite style. "Fortunately, they don't seem at all interested in us."

"The dumpsters out back look promising," I reported. "Lots of pizza boxes and garlicky Chinese take-out containers. We'll have to scout out the neighborhood for liquor stores to raid. We need to lay in supplies for Petey's wedding."

Yes, Phoebe has announced her surprise choice.

"Up yours," replied the despondent groom-to-be.

"That reminds me, Robin," said Honky. "Darla asked me to ask you if we could lay off the plundering for a while."

"Why?" I demanded.

"Well, she seems to think the raids are antagonizing the authorities—you know, that trapping and euthanizing business."

"We *must* smoke and drink, men," I replied. "We owe it to Dr. Milbrene to continue the regimen he imposed. Science demands it."

"Yeah, that's what I told her," said Honky. "She thought maybe we could start up our bar act again."

"Can you mambo on an artificial leg?" I asked.

"I could try," said Honky.

"And should we be captured or killed in the attempt," said Petey, "at least I won't have to choose between the Scylla and Charybdis of fiancées."

Yes, Blanche too has staked a surprise matrimonial claim on our pal. Some guys have all the luck.

* * *

The neighborhood bars, although numerous, proved discouragingly inhospitable to mamboing refreshments seekers. In some the music was so loud we developed an acute weakness in the knees and had to leave immediately. In others oddly dressed Bohemian men seemed more interested in dancing with themselves than watching us perform. Then there was the dimly lit bar where we were nearly trampled by energetic Bohemian women in brawny leather boots.

Despite our continued sobriety, we are feeling pretty good about ourselves. Yesterday we saved a man's life. It happened while we were out patrolling for smokes along the waterfront near a place called Pier 39. We saw a man, possibly a poet, trying to commit suicide by thrusting a long sword down his beak. This was after we had watched, transfixed, as the deranged sonneteer proceeded to light *and eat* several cigarettes. None of the callous onlookers gathered around him was making the slightest effort to prevent this senseless tragedy. Of course, we had to act.

Mr. Gerigar cried, "Good God, man, don't do it!" remembering to add, "Support equal rights for budgies."

Sunny shouted, "You must live to rhyme again!" adding, "Shop wisely: look for the designer label."

Petey and I dive-bombed his head, Kenny dropped a half-eaten halibut down his shirt, and Norris bravely hurled himself against the back of his knees. The despondent poet dropped, struggling, to the pavement. Several onlookers rushed to his aid. After heroic effort, they were able to extract the sword with only minimal shedding of blood. Then the police and ambulances came and we had to leave quickly. No one bothered to thank us, but that's not much of a surprise. We're becoming inured to the callous ways of the city.

* * *

"More negative publicity," sighed Julie, reading the morning paper while seated on her egg.

"What's the headline?" asked Darla.

"Killer Pigeons Attack Street Performer," she replied. "The subhead goes on: Officials Decry Alarming Mayhem from Sky."

"People are idiots," said Petey, smoking one of the last of our Carletombs. "We saved that man's life."

"These outrages must stop," declared Blanche. "After we are married, all smoking and drinking must cease."

"That goes double for me," added Phoebe.

Petey glanced despairingly at me and passed the butt to Honky, who inhaled greedily.

"Did the article mention me?" asked Sunny.

"Doesn't seem to," replied Julie, reading. "Just the Killer Pigeons and a marauding seagull and falcon."

"Little birds never get any respect," complained Sunny. "It's so unfair."

"I respect you, Sunny," said Mr. Gerigar.

"That is all too evident, Bud honey," she replied. "I am still waiting to rebuff your first coarse advance. Francesca would already have slapped you silly."

"She is hardly the ideal role model for you," he replied.

"Evidently not," said Sunny. "I expect you'd prefer that I'd emulate the coolly dispassionate Maltese."

"I never said that."

"There is only one universal tongue," noted Sunny, "the articulate language of the unsaid."

* * *

"Robin, have you seen this passageway?" asked Darla.

"I don't think so," I replied, following her up through the intricate twists and turns of the sherry sign.

"It's my favorite. There are no noisy relays, the wires are all neatly overhead, and see: there are these nice holes you can look through. You can see nearly the entire skyline of downtown."

I peered out through one of the small holes, evidently drilled to afford access to an inner mounting bolt. "Nice view, Darla," I said. "Kind of drafty though."

"But not that bad, Robin. We could stuff some paper over the openings on chilly days. I think this would make a splendid apartment."

"Very nice," I agreed. "We're fortunate Sunny knew about this sign."

"It's so much better than the billboard, Robin. And from here it's just a short hop up to one of the roof openings. So it wouldn't be any trouble bringing in nest materials."

"You're right, Darla, we're near the top of the sign. I can hear Norris up there shmoozing with Maltese."

"Robin, I never told you this, but I think you were extremely brave to go out alone and make contact with that falcon. You could easily have been killed."

"Well, I knew we needed the lifting power of the biggest bird in the city. He's turned out to be a good friend."

"A wonderful friend, Robin. We're lucky to know him—and Kenny too, of course."

"Kenny's a pip."

"Yes, and now it looks like Petey's going to be settling down."

"Does it?" I asked.

"Yes, and Julie told me, confidentially of course, that she finds your friend Honky not unattractive."

"That so, Darla? Well, they're both literary."

"Right. So I was wondering, Robin, if you've ever thought of, of getting settled?"

"How so?"

"Uh . . . domestically, for example."

"Well, I've never told anybody about this, Darla, but I'm in love. I have been for some time."

"Really, Robin?"

"Yes, Darla. Deeply in love."

"Oh, Robin, this is more than I dared hope for."

"Yes, I love Maryanne."

"What?"

"You know, Maryanne from the lab. Used to read to us. She's the one who told us about Mr. Spade."

"Oh, right. That person."

"That's another reason why we have to get back to Berkeley—without delay. I miss her terribly."

"Oh, yes, well. These things take time. . . I suppose."

"Darla! What's that sound?"

"I heard it too, Robin. What was it?"

"Something scraped against the outside of the sign."

"Robin!" screeched Norris overhead. "Maltese is in danger! Come quick!"

I peered out through one of the holes in the sign. The view of downtown was now interrupted by a net of finely woven rope.

Chapter 17

"We're trapped!" shouted Petey, racing up the passageway. "Men have lowered a net from the top of the tower!"

"I'm not going back to Francesca!" cried Sunny, hopping up behind Petey. "I refuse to be trapped day and night in a cage so I can watch that conceited girl have a rich social life."

"Hey, I just remembered what euthanasia is," piped Petey. "It means mercy killing."

"Now you tell us," I muttered. "OK, Petey, go round up the others. Get everything loaded in the trailer. Make sure you get Julie and her egg safely aboard. Darla, you go with Petey."

"Right, Robin," she said.

"Sunny," I said, "where's Kenny?"

"Taking some pizza to his mom, Robbie honey. Pineapple and anchovy I believe he said."

"Damn," I said, bounding up the passageway. I darted through an opening to the top of the sign, and found the alarmed falcon backed up against the tower. Above us, blue-garbed figures leaned out from a tower opening and struggled to secure the all-encircling net. More blue-uniformed men hovered nearby in a noisy craft held aloft by rapidly spinning wings that beat the air like an enormous bee.

"I can't bite through the net!" shouted Norris. "We're trapped. They've bound it tightly against the tower."

I looked around in desperation. "Norris, you've got to drop Maltese. It's our only chance!"

"What?" cried the stricken falcon.

"You've got to throw her off!" I shouted. "The weight might break the net."

"But Robin," he protested, "it's a long way down. Maltese is in no condition to fly."

"Toss her, you stupid bird!" snapped Sunny, darting up behind me. "She's just a dumb statue!"

Norris stared at me questioningly. "Robin, is it . . ."

"It's true," I said. "Throw her! Quick!"

Norris hesitated, then gripped the statuette and heaved it savagely over the side. Light bulbs shattered, sparks flashed, the plummeting figurine hit the bottom of the net and thudded sharply against the tower. Ropes stretched and strained, the net slapped hard against the sign, popping more bulbs. As the men on the roof fought to hold on, the heavy statuette scraped against the concrete, the net sagged . . . but didn't tear.

"Norris, stay here until I come back," I commanded. "Try to keep the men from coming any closer, but don't get your wings snagged in the net!"

He nodded dumbly. I raced back down the passageways, took a wrong turn, got lost, turned in another direction, and at last found my way to the tunnel that led to the trailer.

"Honky," I called, "is Julie aboard?"

"Yes, Robin, with her egg. Mr. Gerigar's in there too trying to get Phoebe and the chicks calmed down."

"Good work. Honky, where's Petey's lighter?"

"In the trailer, under the cat kidneys."

"Get it!" I commanded. "And tell the women to unload all non-essential food items."

"Non-essential in whose opinion?" he demanded.

"We don't have time to argue, Honky. Bring me the lighter!"

"Robin!" called Petey, looking down toward the street from a net-covered opening in the sign, "some sort of big red truck just pulled up and a crew of men climbed out. They're doing something, I can't make out quite what. Oh no, they're extending a ladder—a long one."

I paused, looking at Petey. "Do you think it could be Mr. Spade?"

He returned my gaze. "Uh, well . . . gee, you know . . . probably not."

"Yeah, Petey, probably not."

"Here's the lighter, Robin," said Honky, hurrying toward me with virtually no limp.

Grabbing the lighter, I carried it over to an opening in the sign, flicked the lever, and held the hissing gas flame against the net. The threads of the net smoked—sputtering and charring—but refused to ignite.

"Damn! We need more heat," I said.

"Oh, here, permit me," said Honky.

With his beak he turned a dial on the lighter; a powerful jet of flame shot out from the orifice.

"Good heavens!" I exclaimed.

"Actually, Robin," said Honky, "you were the one who discovered that particular feature—not that I think you remembered it."

I pointed the fiery blast at the net. Liquid fire dripped from the ends as the net strands burned intensely with a smokey black flame. Quickly, I proceeded down the passageway, igniting the net at every opening.

We heard a ripping sound.

"The net's starting to tear!" called Honky.

"There goes Maltese!" shouted Petey.

Each of us watched from a different opening as the statuette tore free and plummeted toward the ground—turning end over end in a stately free fall. The men on the red truck ducked for cover as the black sculpture shattered against the sidewalk in a wave of ricocheting fragments.

"Hurray!" shouted Petey and Honky.

"Get ready, men, to help move out the trailer," I commanded. "I'm going back up for Norris."

I found the falcon and Sunny crouched behind a metal sign panel as the remains of the net burned smokily around them.

"Norris, you'll have to carry the trailer yourself," I said. "We'll try to help you."

"You lied to me, Robin."

"Come on, Norris. I can explain later. We've got to get out of here."

"Why should I help you?"

"Norris, we're your friends. We care about you."

"Maltese fell, Robin," he said dumbly. "She's broken."

"Not to worry, Norrie honey," said Sunny. "She didn't feel a thing. What say, big guy? Let's blow this joint before we all wind up an FBI statistic."

A fragment of concrete blew out above our heads.

"Duck!" I shouted, hitting the deck. More concrete shattered above us, as Sunny and Norris crouched beside me. "My God, they're shooting at us."

"I can see through a crack," said Sunny. "It's the men in that flying machine. They've got guns."

"These guys mean business," I said, as flaming drips from the burning net singed through my feathers and burned my flesh.

"Now they've made me mad," said Norris. "Someone is definitely going to be eaten."

More bullets impacted around us, then the thumping rhythm of the whirling blades abruptly changed as the craft suddenly veered sideways.

"It's Kenny!" shouted Sunny. "He just flew into that machine and decorated the face of the man at the controls with a slice of cold pizza!"

CHAPTER 18

"Are you actually proposing that we reside here?" asked Blanche, gazing about with distaste. "I for one do not intend to begin my married life camped out in a pine tree."

"What married life?" grumbled Petey.

"It's only temporary," I explained. "Kenny promised to scout around for something more suitable. In the meantime this will do as a hideout. I think we're pretty well concealed up here—even Norris and the trailer are well camouflaged."

To escape from the men with guns, we had flown a great distance west to a dense thicket of trees in a broad green area Darla guessed was a park. Below us a small stream, suitable for bathing, burbled from the hillside.

"I did not escape from Francesca's cage to live the life of a rustic bumpkin," said Sunny. "My God, there are bugs in this tree."

"Only little furry brown ones," said Darla. "Robin's right. We must make do for now and not complain."

Phoebe pushed aside her yellow curtains and opened the bedroom window. "Somebody better get that homewrecker out of my trailer before I feed her bastard egg to my kids."

"That's what we'll do," Darla said cheerfully. "We'll build a nice nest for Julie—a real one. Robin, would you like to help?"

"I suppose so," I said wearily. My wings ached, my burns stung painfully, I needed a cigarette and a drink, and I wondered how Mr. Spade would ever find us up here. Would he even bother to look for us now that the Maltese Falcon was destroyed? Never, in all these weeks as a displaced person had I felt such despair.

Honky fluttered in through the bower of thick branches. "Hey, guys, check out this cigarette I just scored. It's most unusual."

* * *

Nest building. A challenge in applied geometry. You gather a twig here, a piece of string there, perhaps a bit of fluff from your own downy nethers. Sniggering, you mug your local falcon for a feather or two. Pile it on. Tuck it in. Cosmic. You take another drag on Honky's exquisite cigarette. Wow, that's intense. You ponder your crude adumbration. More twigs! More fluff! You will build a nest that will live for a thousand years. A nest of engorged fecundity. A nest to swaddle the fruit of your fervid genes. You pause, suddenly attuned to your own borborygmus. Why stop with a nest? Why not a cathedral of twigs? An amphitheater of fluff? A megalopolis of detritus?

"It's a wonderful thing, a wonderful thing," said Petey, stepping back to admire our handiwork.

"It's an offering to the sacred Earth Mother," declared Honky, beginning to weep softly.

"It looks like a tumbleweed that blew in off a trash pile," observed Blanche.

"Oh, I think it will do," said Darla. "We'll just straighten it up a bit. It's certainly big."

The same, alas, could not be said for Honky's magical cigarette. It had dwindled to nothing, like an evanescent imagined enchantment.

* * *

Not a pleasant night. The furry brown bugs grew ever more numerous and a bone-chilling fog settled upon us. There is also the issue of Norris, who seems to have sunk into a black depression. It is more than a little nervous-making living in close proximity to a morose falcon. He sulked for hours after Darla suggested as gently as she could that he not leave the tree until it was safely dark. Then he dragged back and devoured some sort of powerfully odoriferous black and white cat. He wouldn't share it either, muttering that we were all lucky he wasn't dining on pigeon instead. So even though we were unusually ravenous, we had to make do with some stale fortune cookies that Kenny found in a dumpster behind a Chinese restaurant. My fortune read, "You will live a life of sumptuous luxury." Somewhat ironic to contemplate as I shivered on a damp pine branch and plucked creepy bugs out of my feathers.

The coverage in the morning newspaper was the most sensational so far. The enormous black headline read, "Bullets Fly as Killer Pigeons Evade Police Dragnet." A sidebar added, "Fierce Fusillade Damages Heritage Sign." It seems our cozy sign was some sort of national historic landmark. And I thought it was just a big advertisement for booze. Next to a photo of the bullet-riddled sign was an unflattering police-artist sketch of the beleaguered victims of the unprovoked assault—us.

"Hmmm," said Petey, studying the drawing. "They've got Honky's peg on the wrong foot. And who's that grossly obese character?"

"Why that's you," replied Honky. "A pretty good likeness too."

In a gesture that could hardly be characterized as "tolerant of eccentrics" the city is now offering a reward of $10,000 for our capture—dead or alive.

"Dead," noted Mr. Gerigar. "That seems rather extreme."

"Except as a description of my lovelife," commented Sunny.

"Since when is borrowing the occasional cigarette a capital offense?" demanded Petey.

"If anything, you're doing people a favor taking away those toxic things," said Julie from her sprawling ramshackle nest—no longer the object of its builders' unalloyed pride.

The news article also quoted the pilot of the police helicopter (flying machine) as saying he would not rest until the felonious seagull who attacked him was brought to justice.

"Hey, he started it by shooting at you guys," said Kenny, puffing on a cigarette he had just swiped on nearby Haight street, source of Honky's magic smoke. He passed it to Honky.

"Damn, it's just an ordinary Lordylard," complained Honky. "Kenny, did you steal it from a young guy dressed in black with long head feathers?"

"Yeah, Honky. Just like you told me. But all the young guys on that street wear black clothes and have long head feathers."

* * *

We have found a partial solution for the creepy little bug problem. We collect them into small piles and shovel them down the throats of little Wallace Junior and baby Ina. So far no ill effects, and it's taken the pressure off the overworked food gatherers. Only Darla, Blanche, Phoebe, and Kenny dare venture out of the tree during daylight hours. To cheer up the grieving falcon, Sunny has been recounting lurid tales of the amorous adventures of Francesca's more uninhibited friends. I'm not sure that's such a good idea. Mr. Gerigar suggested intensive counseling, but Norris refused, citing the therapist's all-too-obvious failure with his last client.

To pass the time, we've been working our way through numerous cigarettes retrieved by Kenny. No more winners, but we've been enjoying the plentiful smokes. Sobriety continues unabated; Darla has requested in her forceful way that Kenny stay out of liquor stores. As a consequence, Petey has stated that with no sherry to dull his reason and weaken his inhibitions he will be unable to enter into any matrimonial engagements at this time. I pray Phoebe doesn't grow impatient and dragoon some other unfortunate person into a marital entanglement.

The pine boughs parted, and Darla and Blanche hopped in looking as pale as it is possible for persons fully covered in feathers to appear.

"Robin, we've made a gruesome discovery," gasped Darla. "I think there's been a murder!"

* * *

A murder! Unfortunate for the victim, but just the thing to distract an aspiring detective from his desperate circumstances. I set to work at once on the case: interrogating the two shaken women on what they had seen, discussing the matter with my associates, alerting Norris and Kenny to stand by, and pacing back and forth among the crawling bugs as I waited impatiently for night to fall.

At last, it was dark enough to venture forth.

"Robin, do be careful," said Darla.

"Yes, Honky," cautioned Julie from her nest. "Please don't take any unnecessary chances."

"That goes for you too, Petey," added Blanche. "And stay out of the bars."

Following the route specified by Darla, we soon spotted the suspicious white van (box on wheels) parked next to a padlocked dumpster behind a nondescript wooden building. We alighted on a nearby roof to study the scene.

"I hate it when they put locks on our food," said Petey.

"It's so unfair," agreed Honky. "I always assume there's something especially delectable in there when I see a lock."

"It smells like something large and unwashed died quite some time ago," noted Sunny.

"Yes, it's most appetizing," replied Petey.

"Very clever," I said. "The killer parked the van next to the dumpster so people would think the odor was coming from the garbage."

"I wonder if the body is still in the vehicle?" said Mr. Gerigar.

"No one seems to be around," I said. "Let's go investigate."

We flew down and hovered laboriously above the small square windows high in the rear doors of the dented van.

"Do you see anything?" I panted.

"I see some legs!" cried Sunny.

"My God, the corpse has been savagely dismembered," gasped Petey, struggling to stay airborne.

"Odd thing though," said Mr. Gerigar. "One of the legs is white and the other appears to be brown."

Multiple murders!

"I hope the white leg is not Brigid O'Shaughnessy's," said Honky.

"I doubt her slim, shapely calf is quite that muscular," I replied. Feeling faint from exertion, I glided down and landed in the deep shadows under the van; the others quickly joined me.

"We've got to get inside," I said.

"I don't see how, Robin," said Kenny. "All the windows are rolled up tight."

"Look!" said Sunny, pointing upward. "There's a damaged section in the metal underside. It appears to be rusted all the way through."

"Good work, Sunny," I said. "Now what I want you to do is squeeze in through that opening and inspect the bodies."

"In your dreams," replied the parakeet. She turned to her would-be significant other. "Bud honey, do you want to make your best girl proud of you?"

"Oh, very well," he sighed. "I suppose there's no one else."

The small bird flew up and bravely wormed his way through the jagged opening.

"Good gracious," we heard him exclaim. "There's a big pile of legs in here. And arms too!"

"What's an arm?" asked Honky.

"I think he's referring to wings," I replied. "Mr. Gerigar, can you work the latch on the door?"

"I'm trying," he replied. "But I don't have enough strength."

We all turned expectantly toward Sunny.

"Oh, all right," she said. "But it's very ungentlemanly of you to ask."

Sunny flew up and disappeared through the hole. A moment later we heard the latch on one of the back doors click open. As Kenny and Norris tugged on the handle, a leg tumbled out and clattered across the concrete—narrowly missing Petey. We gathered 'round this grisly relic of a heinous crime.

"Rigor mortis has obviously set in," I said, tapping gingerly on the stiff naked limb.

"A neat surgical cut at the knee," noted Petey. "No blood at all."

"We're obviously dealing with a professional," I replied.

"One with unsettling proclivities," said Honky. "Look, he's removed all the inner contents of the limb."

"Probably ate it with relish," said Norris enviously.

I walked over to the severed end of the leg and peered into its dark, cavernous interior. "It's been painstakingly hollowed out," I exclaimed, my voice echoing eerily from its anatomical depths. "It's the work of a depraved fiend!"

"Or perhaps a despicable ghoul," suggested Honky.

"Oh, you're all nuts," said Sunny, hopping up on the evidence. "This isn't a real leg. It's fake!"

"What a bother," said Petey. "She's right."

* * *

Of course, we're all happy for the many victims who weren't viciously slain and cruelly dismembered by the leg-hollowing killer. Still, Sunny's revelation came as something of a disappointment to me. I'm sure Mr. Spade would have felt the same had it happened on his first big case.

"Honky, what's that lettering on the side of the van?" I asked.

"Uh, it says: Trinello's Mannequin Exchange. Repairs - Renovations - Transplants."

"What's a mannequin?" asked Kenny.

"I don't know," said Petey. "It must be some sort of artificial person."

"Why would anyone want an artificial person?" asked Honky. "Aren't there more than enough real people already?"

"It does seem suspicious," I said.

"Oh, I don't know," said Sunny. "Some folks may prefer a measure of artificiality in their friends. Right, Norris?"

"Could be," he replied. "Just as they might prefer a nice parakeet appetizer if they haven't eaten all day."

"How fortunate no one has ever called me nice," she replied.

"Gee, I wonder if Mr. Trinello has a spare mannequin leg in my size," said Honky, peering into the moonlit van. "I could use one with a real foot."

"I'm sure they don't," said Mr. Gerigar, looking about anxiously. "Perhaps we should leave before somebody comes."

"Wait," I said. "This leg appears to be of a light, yet substantial construction."

"So?" said Petey.

"So, we happen to be in need of some sturdy, weather-resistant housing. Norris, could you carry this limb?"

"Sure, Robin," he said. "But I'm not going to fall in love with it."

"Not a leg man, huh?" winked Sunny. "Ken honey, how about grabbing one of those nice arms for Bud and me?"

"Should I, Robin?" he asked.

"An excellent idea," I said. "A wing would be just the right size to house two parakeets."

"Not that arm, Ken dear," said Sunny. "I could never feel comfortable in a home with an outstretched finger pointing so accusingly. I might develop a severe case of guilt by association."

* * *

A strange night. Flying home in the moonlight, we kept hearing screams from below. Residents of both sexes appeared to be going through some sort of violent emotional tumult. Especially blood-curdling were the screams of solitary pedestrians on Haight Street as we flew along low in a fruitless search for Honky's long-feathered, black-garbed smoker. We had to settle for the usual assortment of richly satisfying yet unmagical commercial brands, discarded in panic by fleeing smokers. I wonder what all the commotion was about?

We lodged the leg in a crotch of the pine tree; the wing we wedged in some branches above Phoebe's trailer.

"A most fortuitous find," commented Darla, inspecting our new communal home. "This leg is quite roomy and we can store food items in the foot."

"Perhaps we could persuade a woodpecker to put in some windows," suggested Julie from her nest.

"Let's hope so," said Blanche. "Otherwise it could get awfully stuffy in there."

"Oh, I think it will be fine," said Julie. "And I'm glad no one was murdered after all. You fellows are to be commended for solving that mystery."

"Here's something odd," said Darla, emerging from the leg. "I found this feather in the toe."

"Let me see that," said Julie. "Why, it's my feather!"

"How can it be?" I said. "You haven't been off your nest since we got back. Are you sure it's yours?"

"A girl knows her own feather when she sees it," she replied. "See, it's my lovely shade of dove grey."

Julie held the feather up to her breast; the match was perfect.

"You know," said Petey, "the vehicle we were kidnapped in was a white van."

"You're right, Petey," said Darla. "That's why I flew down to inspect that van when I spotted it."

"What does all this mean?" asked Julie.

"It means," I said, "that we must find this Mr. Trinello and investigate him. This could be the break we've been waiting for."

"What's that noise?" hissed Honky.

"It's coming from close by," whispered Darla.

"I recognize that repellent racket," declared Blanche. "It's the sounds of drunken carousing!"

CHAPTER 19

And so three more long-lost colleagues joined us in our tree-top anatomical domicile, christened "Mi Calfa" by Petey. Our tipsy guests are Zeb, Jasper, and Yancy of the celebrated Test Group D.

"It's not a bad little house," said Zeb, dazzling the ladies with his film-star looks. "Not bad if you're obliged to live in a tree. But that falcon pal of yours gave us quite a start."

"Are you sure he can be trusted?" asked Jasper, his thin neck twitching as he spoke.

"Perfectly," I replied. "Norris has given us his word he won't eat anyone. He's still tormented with remorse for eating poor Wallace by mistake."

"Who's Wallace?" asked Yancy, a stocky fellow with coarse, mottled feathers.

"Wallace was our cagemate who lived with that pigeon you met in the trailer," explained Honky. "Julie is incubating his egg."

"Wallace laid an egg?" asked Yancy, impressed.

"*I* laid the egg," explained Julie from her nest, newly relocated to the mannequin ankle. "Wallace, er, engendered it."

A period of embarrassed feet-shuffling ensued. I contemplated the furry bugs making themselves at home on the moonlit leg opening.

"So, what have you fellows been drinking?" inquired Petey. "I don't recognize that aroma on your breath."

"It's beer!" exhaled Yancy. "Wonderful stuff."

"Very calming to the nerves," twitched Jasper, not looking at all calm.

"Sounds delightful," said Honky. "And where does one obtain beer?"

No answer. None.

"Uh, we've been raiding liquor stores," I said, breaking the awkward silence. "Norris and Kenny, our seagull buddy, are most adept at securing sherry, but we've had to lay low recently."

"Yeah, I know," said Zeb. "The heat's been pretty intense. We were having an innocent smoke in Union Square yesterday when some bozos in blue tried to throw a net over us."

"What happened?" asked Darla.

"We got away," he replied. "The fat lady with the Pigeon Chow concession attacked them with her signs. I think she was protesting something. So they tied her up by her wings and dragged her away."

"That's terrible!" exclaimed Darla.

"I can't believe you people used to eat that awful stuff she peddles," said Jasper.

"Give me a bag of fried pork rinds any day," added Yancy.

"Yes, we read about your mugging that tot," said Honky.

"We didn't mug him," twitched Jasper. "We only swiped the little snitch's snacks."

"I believe that falls under the usual definition of a mugging," noted Petey.

"I wish I was back at the lab," said Yancy. "What a life that was."

"We're desperate to get back as well," I said. "We've been doing everything we can think of to find a way."

"Yancy has a special reason for wanting to go back," remarked Zeb.

"Oh, what's that, Zeb?" asked Darla.

"He's got the hots for one of the lab assistants," answered Jasper. "Right, Yanc'?"

"You know it, Jasp'," he replied. "Maybe you dudes remember her—a hot blonde tamale by the name of Maryanne. What a babe!"

I suddenly felt ill. And it wasn't from the bug crawling up my leg.

* * *

I can see why the trend in newspaper readership is down. Every time Kenny brings back the morning paper, my wings start to shake and I'm gripped by powerful sherry cravings. For example, this morning's banner black headline read: "Killer Pigeons on Murderous Rampage."

"Good gracious, Zeb," I exclaimed, "did you fellows murder someone for their beer?"

"Of course not," he replied. "But last night I heard your falcon buddy snapping some poor wretch's bones."

"Norris," I called, "did you by any chance abduct and eat a person?"

"Why no," he replied, waking from his slumbers. "Let's see, what did I eat last night? Oh yes, tiring of cat, I decided to try one of those shaggy animals that people are always dragging around on chains. I obtained one of the compact models as a sample."

"How was it?" asked Yancy.

"Extremely delicious," said Norris. "I ate everything except the tail, the rhinestone collar, and the little metal tags."

"According to this article," said Honky, scanning the front page, "the homicidal birds were seen in the vicinity of Haight Street near Buena Vista Park. Multiple witnesses reported seeing them carrying the bloody remains of a dismembered corpse."

"Well, we were on Haight Street," I said. "But I don't recall seeing any homicidal birds."

"Yes, but Norris and Kenny also were there," Darla pointed out. "And they were transporting the leg and wing."

"Completely artificial," I replied. "That much has been firmly established. These are mannequin parts from the highly suspicious Mr. Trinello, who we'll be investigating as soon as Kenny gets back with my drink."

"This is a blunder," said Zeb gravely. "A serious blunder."

"I might have known it," said Blanche. "Smoking, drinking, and now this: implicated in a shocking murder. Petey, what do you have to say for yourself?"

Petey roused himself and ruffled his feathers. "Where's Kenny with that damn drink?"

I suppose I should take heart from the example of Mr. Spade. You can't really call yourself a professional dick in this town unless the authorities are trying to pin at least one murder rap on you.

At that moment the seagull returned—empty-footed. "Police cars all around the park!" Kenny shouted. "Men are unrolling big nets!"

* * *

Another day, another desperate flight for our lives. As Sunny points out, if our community of refugees gets any larger, we'll have to charter a city bus to effect our escapes. We hurriedly transferred Julie's egg and as much of her disorderly nest as we could to Phoebe's trailer. Of course, we had to abandon our cozy "Mi Calfa" and wing. Darla is confident they will be discovered by the authorities, who will realize their error and retract that ridiculous charge of murder. I hope so.

Zeb insisted on leading the way as Norris and Kenny hauled the heavily laden trailer. The rest of us trailed forlornly behind, dodging the occasional sharpshooters' bullets. Thank goodness we were able to evade the police helicopter. I was not surprised to observe that uncouth Yancy was a crude, graceless flyer.

Zeb contends the way to escape detection is to avoid public places and seek refuge among the city's affluent citizens. He says the police tread very lightly around the privileged classes. No gunplay or unnecessary roughness allowed. So Zeb has brought us to some sort of walled estate at the top of a hill across the street from a tranquil green park. We're in a posh neighborhood called Pacific Heights.

The main house is a monster: all pink stone and monumental columns. We're ensconced at the bottom of the lushly landscaped garden in what Petey identified as an old carriage house. Entry to the deserted attic was obtained via the application by Norris of a brick to a small window up under the eaves in back. The attic is dark and creepy, but well sheltered from the weather and extremely private. No bugs except for a few reclusive spiders which Phoebe promptly fed to Wally Junior. We put the trailer down on a dusty cardboard box and set about making ourselves at home as best we could.

"Where would you like your nest, Julie?" asked Darla.

"Oh, I think on that shelf next to that pretty pennant."

"What does it say?" asked Jasper, still twitching rapidly from the police gunfire.

Julie studied the ornate red and gold letters, descending in size as the faded banner narrowed to a point. "Let's see, it says: Souvenir of the Panama-Pacific International Exhibition, 1915."

"Darn, looks like we missed it," said Honky.

"Wow, this is pretty swank," exclaimed Sunny, hopping up on the window sill. "There's a very pricey view of the bay and distant Tiburon. Bud honey, we've joined the social elite."

"What's that big artificial pond?" he asked.

"That's not a pond, Bud dear. It's our own private swimming pool and spa. I feel like I'm on my honeymoon!"

"Me too," said Phoebe, looking accusingly at Petey.

"As do I," noted Blanche for the record.

* * *

"Petey, what are birds of prey?" I asked, puffing on a Newmort.

"Birds of prey, hmm," he said. "Well, obviously, they are birds associated with some theological discipline. I expect they are deeply devout."

"I see," I replied. "Then it seems the police have given up on their nets and guns, and now intend to send proselytizing birds after us."

"Yep, that's what it says here," confirmed Honky, perusing the afternoon paper, hot off the press. The immense black-bordered headline bellowed: "Killer Pigeons Escape Again!"

"No doubt these religious birds are infused with the customary tiresome missionary zeal," said Petey. "Be assured, their dogma holds no terrors for me. I am prepared to challenge them tenet by tenet."

"Good for you, Petey," I replied. "Honky, is there no mention of the police finding the mannequin parts?"

"None whatsoever," he replied. "What does this mean?"

"It means Mr. Spade is right," I sighed. "The police are complete incompetents. We'll have to return to the pine tree and do their job for them."

"Damn," said Petey. "Oh well, would you care to gamble on another rice roll?"

"No, thanks, I'm stuffed," I replied.

We were dining at a back-alley dumpster in an architecturally eccentric district called Japantown, a short flight down the hill from our palatial new hideout. If you were lucky, you found at the center of your rice roll a morsel of extremely undercooked fish. If you were less fortunate, you encountered marginally edible matter that defied identification. If luck deserted you, a spicy bomb of powdery green stuff detonated in your nose and knocked you on your tail feathers.

"Robin, what did you say to Kenny as we were leaving?" asked

Petey.

"I instructed him to follow Zeb and his pals if they went anywhere. I'm not sure we can trust those fellows."

"Maybe we should ask the tot-muggers to leave," suggested Honky.

"We can't," insisted Petey. "We need those men. I'm planning on marrying Yancy off to Phoebe. And I think Jasper is an ideal catch for Blanche."

"How about Zeb for Julie?" asked Honky.

"Nah," replied Petey. "He's putting the moves on Darla."

"Don't be silly," I said. "They hardly know each other."

"Love is blind," whistled Honky.

"You're just imagining things," I retorted. "Darla would never be impressed by a flashy character like Zeb. She's much too sensible."

"Time will tell," said Petey, contributing another cliche to the irritating topic.

"Here's something interesting," said Honky, studying the paper. "It's about those furry little bugs. It says there's an infestation of Fubsy Bugs in the city parks."

"Fubsy Bugs, huh?" I said, appreciating the change of subject.

"That's right," said Honky. "And according to entomologists the Fubsy is not a beetle, but is in fact a true bug."

"Well, that's a relief," noted Petey. "I'd hate to think our Wally Junior and baby Ina were eating beetles."

"Hey, Scotty! It's the Killer Pigeons!"

We looked up from our Japanese lunch. Two plaid-shirted men, possibly tourists, had wandered down the alley to relieve themselves.

"What makes you say that, Danny?" asked the other man, releasing a vigorous stream.

After some fumbling, Danny commenced his own gushing discharge. "Well, there's the white one with the gold peg leg, the chubby one, and the red one."

"I don't see any falcons though," said Scotty, shaking his nozzle to reinvigorate the flow.

"I tell you, Scotty, there's a $10,000 reward out for these buzzards. Hand me your cell phone quick. I'm calling 911."

"I can't hand you my cell phone, Danny. I'm processing four double sakis and about a gallon of green tea."

"How fatiguing," I said. "Let's go men."

We flew home to the hideout—taking a circuitous route to prevent our being tailed by birds of prey. Violence I was prepared to deal with; religion was another matter entirely.

* * *

"I tell you they're drunk!" insisted Blanche.

"We don't know that for certain, Blanche," said Darla. "Zeb merely expressed a desire to take a nap."

Lined up motionless on a shelf above Julie's nest, Zeb and his buddies had swiveled their necks around and buried their heads deep in their wing feathers. In the fading light they resembled three fluffy decapitated mannequins. I leaned toward the repugnant Yancy and sniffed. The yeasty odor of beer was unmistakable.

"Yes, they're probably just napping," I lied.

"Uh, I don't think so, Robin," said Kenny.

"Kenny, I'll take your report privately," I replied. "Has everyone eaten?"

"Everyone except Norris," said Darla. "As usual he'll be grabbing something after dark."

"The garbage cans were even more wonderful than we'd dared hope," said Julie from her nest. "You wouldn't believe the delicacies they discard."

"Did you see anyone from the house?" I asked.

"Two boys came out," reported Mr. Gerigar. "They were bouncing some sort of ball."

"It's such a shame," said Sunny. "All that money and they were wasting precious shopping hours tossing a ball through a metal loop on a pole. It's true: wealth is wasted on the rich."

"Materialism is no route to personal fulfillment," declared Mr. Gerigar.

"Well, Bud honey," Sunny replied, "when you decide to pursue another route, do let me know. In the meantime, I'd settle for a charge card from Nordstrom's."

* * *

Excusing ourselves, we departed with feigned nonchalance and followed our seagull spy to the site of his afternoon discovery. Less than two blocks away, in a well-cloistered garden behind another imposing home, under a cloth roof suspended on four metal poles, on a large overturned tin tub, sat a silvery metal barrel, smelling invitingly of beer.

"How does it work, Kenny?" asked Petey as we all fluttered down to the tub.

"Well, Petey, from what I could see, it's a lot easier than holding up liquor stores. One of us has to sit on that lever. Then the rest of us gather underneath and catch the foamy liquid as it drips out."

An unexpected test for altruism. We looked at each other. No volunteers stepped forward.

"With my handicap," said Honky, "I couldn't possibly balance on that lever."

"Me neither," said Petey. "I wouldn't have the strength."

"I'm much too big," said Kenny. "I might bust it."

"Oh, all right," I said. "But save some for me."

We had a beer party. A wonderful party. Petey contrived to jam a stick in the lever. Much beer was consumed. Oceans of creamy rich beer. We did not go back to the pine tree. We did not investigate Mr. Trinello. We did not discuss theology with birds of prey. We did not upbraid the tot-muggers for their irresponsible behavior. Later, much later, we found our way back to the hideout, tucked our heads under our wings, and took naps. Long ones.

CHAPTER 20

Many days have passed. Were I more mathematically inclined, I'd tell you the precise number. I was attempting to keep track, but enthusiastic beer consumption seems to cause unexplained gaps in one's internal calendar. I suppose a sharp detective could count the cigarette butts on the attic floor and divide that figure by the average smoked per day to arrive at a close approximation. Unfortunately, fastidious Darla periodically gathers up the accumulated butts and tosses them over the back garden wall. If one calculated at what intervals she performs this housekeeping task, one could plug that statistic into the formula, but as I mentioned before I am not mathematically inclined.

A deep chill has settled over our relationship with the totmuggers. I attribute this in part to their boorishness and in part to the recent exhaustion of our communal beer supply. The silvery barrel (called a "keg" by Zebulon) is empty. Of course, we are keeping a discreet watch over it in hopes it will be replaced or refilled. So far, it has been sadly neglected by the inattentive householder. As Darla forbids liquor store raids and frowns on daytime excursions from the attic, we have been cooped up in a state of irritable sobriety. Several nasty pecks have been given and received, even among friends.

Despite this enforced proximity, the lumpen Jasper and Yancy have failed to take advantage of numerous opportunities to woo marriage-minded females. Meanwhile, bossy Zeb continues to engage Darla in long, possibly intimate conversations. Lately he has been inviting her out for evening garbage raids—just the two of them. I am sorry to report that she has not put the cad firmly in his place by repulsing his crude overtures. Instead, she gives every sign of enjoying his loathsome attentions!

Several boxes of old clothing have been uncovered, no doubt outmoded finery discarded by past generations of mansion residents. Most of the contents are much too big, but Sunny and others have enjoyed dressing up in the more manageable handkerchiefs, silk scarves, lace panties, etc. Today the fashion-minded parakeet chewed a hole in the toe of a white embroidered sock and is presently modeling it as a caftan. Phoebe has adopted a zigzag-patterned man's sock as a shoulder wrap. The clashing colors do cover up some of her bald patches.

Julie continues to sit patiently on her egg. Can it be that such an extended gestation period is the rule laid down by nature? Phoebe has hinted that the egg is unfertile—sired by hysterical jealousy, not our late cagemate. A cruel suggestion that Julie is bravely ignoring. I hope it's not true.

More bad news: When we returned to Buena Vista Park, we discovered the mannequin leg and wing were gone. Two depressions in the soft ground, aligned on an axis perpendicular to the trunk, indicated to me that a ladder-like device had been employed to gain access to the upper branches. It couldn't have been the police because we would have read about it in the newspapers. Petey theorizes it was Mr. Trinello, but I believe the mannequin parts were discovered by Sam Spade. How unfortunate that the master detective arrived just a short time after we had departed. Another disturbing development: Mr. Trinello's white van is nowhere to be found. There is some good news: at least we've been spared tedious visitations by birds of prey.

We are enjoying the spa. The pool is too scary and deep to

venture into, but every evening after midnight we gather in the shallows of the spa for a bracing hot bath. I love to soak in the steamy vapors while enjoying a nice smoke. Then we peck through the luxurious garbage, check hopefully on the beer barrel, and survey the neighborhood for suspicious mannequin renovators. Sometimes we rendezvous on an out-of-the-way rooftop to share a bottle retrieved by Norris from Where We Dare Not Ask. If only Maryanne were there to enjoy it with me. I long to taste a dry imported sherry on her sweet beak. And I wouldn't mind seeing the expression on Yancy's ugly face either as I sweep her up in my manly wings.

* * *

"Isn't it exciting?" cooed Sunny. "They're getting ready for a party!"

"How do you know that?" asked Mr. Gerigar.

"Well, Bud honey, the signs are obvious. There are fresh flowers in all the public rooms, the children have been banished to the upper floors, handsome waiters are setting out bottles of chilled champagne on linen-draped tables, and Mrs. M's gown and coiffure are even more stunningly elegant than usual."

Mrs. M is Sunny's name for the mistress of the mansion in whose garden we are laying low. Sunny spends her days spying on this glamorous family from an abandoned birdhouse in a tree overhanging the back terrace. From her clandestine perch, the envious parakeet can indulge her obsessive fascination with the lifestyles of the materially over-endowed.

The occupants of the house, she reports, include nine children of assorted ages and sexes, several servants, a myopic elderly gardener, and Mrs. M. No husband, says Sunny, but several suitors have been catalogued, of whom Sunny prefers the tall distinguished one who sneaks a drink from the bar whenever Mrs. M leaves the room. An older woman, first thought to be Mrs. M's mother, has been reclassified as the maid, since—among other things—the woman is brown and Mrs. M is white. The gardener is a shade in between. All the children are white except for the oldest girl, who sits nearly nude under a bright lamp and is almost as dark as the maid. The purpose of this activity eludes us, but Sunny suspects it may be a form of punishment, since mother and daughter are often seen exchanging heated words.

Fortunately for us, the children have mostly avoided the garden since its recent invasion by Fubsy Bugs. The tots have ceased their endless wanderings among the shrubbery while plaintively bellowing "Sparky!" at the tops of their little lungs. Apparently, Sparky was some sort of family pet who disappeared suddenly.

When the bugs first appeared, Mrs. M herself strolled down in clinging, bias-cut lilac garments and yelled at the old stooped-over gardener whose name is Miguel. He sprayed some noxious vapors from a red metal can, causing a large cloud of swooning Fubsy Bugs to fall dead into the swimming pool. More yelling resulted from this toxic mishap. Meanwhile, the bugs grow ever more numerous.

"What sort of party do you suppose it is?" asked Darla.

"It's a fund-raising party," reported Sunny. "One of the waiters mentioned it when he was bringing in the hors d'oeuvres."

"What's a fund-raising party?" asked Blanche.

"It's a wonderful innovation," replied Sunny. "I only wish I'd thought of it. Whenever your funds are running low—say you splurged a little too much at Neiman's—you invite a bunch of people over, have a swell time, then put the bite on them."

"They give you money?" asked Phoebe, incredulous.

"Well, not to you, Phoebe honey," said Sunny. "You do have to be glamorous and charming."

* * *

The fund-raising party is in full swing. Under the cover of darkness, we have stolen out of our attic hideout to observe the festivities from Sunny's tree. Many handsome and tastefully garbed guests are in attendance, including all of Mrs. M's known suitors.

Sunny is optimistically predicting duels in the garden before mid-night. I hope the jealous combatants choose swords instead of pistols. At least Mrs. M is not playing favorites; she seems to have kissed everyone (or the air in their vicinity) except her maid and the waiters. But I suppose one cannot maintain a haughty reserve when perilously overdrawn at Neiman's.

I can see how this party strategy is conducive to the free offer-ing of funds. What with the lively conversation, pleasant music, tantalizingly aromatic eats, and trays of sparkling drinks borne by white-jacketed waiters, even I might feel tempted to open my wallet if I had one.

"Isn't this fun?" asked Zeb, intruding rudely upon Darla's cher-ished solitude.

"It's enchanting, Zeb," she replied. "It's the first real party I've ever been to."

"I can't think of anyone I'd rather share it with than you," the cad replied.

"Why, Zeb, how sweet," said Darla, too polite to tell him to drop dead.

"Jasper," hissed Petey, "why don't you go ask Blanche if she'd like to dance?"

"Up yours," replied the twitching party-pooper.

Petey hopped over to a branch occupied by loathsome Yancy. "Psst," whispered the matchmaker, "there's Phoebe alone in the moonlight."

"She can stay that way too," replied the speckled lout. "I wouldn't date that pigeon on a bet."

Just then, a tall glass-paned door opened, and Mrs. M strolled out onto the stone terrace in the company of a stylishly dressed figure familiar to every San Franciscan—even homeless abductees from Berkeley.

"Wonderful party," said the mayor.

"Thank you, your honor. Oh dear, more of those dreadful bugs! My beautiful garden is being devoured."

"We're working on it," he said, flicking a bug from her silken sleeve. "But you know the reaction when anyone proposes using pesticides—especially city-wide. Screams of outrage from all the tree-huggers and then they expect me to swig a highball glass of it to prove it's safe. Hell, if it were safe, it wouldn't kill the bugs."

"I suppose so," she sighed. "And what of those awful Killer Pigeons. Have you identified the victim of their murderous assault?"

"Well, just between you, me, and the Fubsy Bugs, it wasn't quite a murder."

"What?"

"No, I'm told the detectives found some artificial limbs up in a tree."

"You mean prosthetic devices?"

"Something like that, I gather."

"Oh dear, how embarrassing," she said, gripping his arm.

"We're keeping it under wraps. We figure the more outraged the citizenry, the more likely the birds will be discovered and their whereabouts reported."

"I'm going to eat him," said Norris, shocked. "I've never eaten a mayor, but I believe it is now my civic duty to do so."

* * *

I persuaded Norris to delay all acts of revenge until after the party. The male members of our community and Sunny gathered on the roof of the front portico as the guests were departing. We observed the mayor give Mrs. M a small white envelope (presumably his funds payoff), watched as he climbed into his oddly extended black car, then followed behind as the car made its way downhill through nearly deserted streets. After a thankfully brief journey, the car stopped in front of a tall building with ornate arched windows jutting out in orderly bays.

The rear car door opened, the mayor stepped out, Kenny sailed out of the darkness and neatly relieved him of his hat, then Norris descended talons-first on his exposed, featherless head. The mayor cried out, Petey and I rushed forward to peck his hosiery-clad ankles, and Honky goosed him vigorously from the rear. The tot-muggers were deployed to harass the driver, who quickly ducked back into the car — slamming the door on the mayor's outstretched wingtips. Loud shrieking from His Honor.

The door re-opened and the driver emerged waving a large bath-water rain stick. Petey and I administered a departing bite, Norris extracted one more tuft of graying mayoral fringe, Honky delivered a final poke, and we hastily retreated to a nearby pole.

The mayor groaned and clutched his injured wingtips as the driver spoke urgently into a small device connected by a coiled wire to the car's control panel.

"You are a disgrace to your office," scolded Mr. Gerigar from the roof of a nearby car. "My cousin is a successful orthodontist in Hillsborough."

"I hope that smarts tremendously," added Sunny. "Cool mauves and teals are the exciting new colors for the spring fashion sea-son."

The parakeets lit out for an upper bay window (and we did the same) as a police car roared up the street and screeched to a halt. Two blue-uniformed men leaped out to assist the mayor, as another man climbed out slowly from the back seat. Poised on the man's gloved left wing was a large bird.

"What's that, Robin?" asked Kenny, still clutching the mayor's black fedora.

"I believe it may be a bird of prey," I cautioned.

"You're right," said Petey. "It seems to be wearing some sort of priest's vestments."

The man unlaced and removed from the bird's head what appeared to be a black leather priest's hood.

"My God, it's a falcon!" I exclaimed.

"That's no priest," gasped Norris, peering down intently. "That's a nun!"

CHAPTER 21

The nun's name is Angelina, although I suppose the proper form of address would be Sister Angelina. She is of such a size as to inspire reverential awe—even larger than Norris if you can believe it. After Norris hastily introduced himself, she released Jasper from the death grip in which she was clutching him, and accepted an invitation to return with us to our secluded attic hideout. On the way I took Norris aside and stressed that he must pretend to no small measure of piety if he was to impress his new-found friend.

Taking my suggestion to heart, Brother Norris said a brief prayer before we launched into a gala welcoming feast. The menu included discarded party canapes, fresh cat, Fubsy Bugs (for the youngsters), and expensive French champagne laboriously salvaged from a legion of bottles hauled out to the alley by Miguel.

"It's not Friday is it?" asked Norris, pausing theatrically with his first furry helping of cat.

"No, it's Saturday," sighed Sunny. "We just missed White Flower Day at Macys."

"I always abstain from meat on Fridays," Norris lied.

"This cat is wonderful," said Angelina. "I've never had it before."

"What are you accustomed to eating?" asked Zeb, offering a curried lobster canape to Darla, as if she were paralyzed and incapable of helping herself.

"Rodents mostly," the nun replied, sipping her champagne. "Sometimes small wild birds. Or pigeons."

Phoebe gave a start; Jasper twitched anew.

"Oh, excuse me," said Angelina.

"That's all right," said Norris. "No one can live an entirely spiritual life. The body—as well as the soul—requires sustenance."

"Uh, right," she said.

"So you were trained to attack when commanded by the fellow with the glove?" asked Petey.

"That's correct," she replied. "It wasn't a bad life. He was kind to me. But it was rather lonely."

She glanced shyly at Norris, who smiled in sympathy.

"For a bird of your convictions, it must have been a grueling test of your faith," he said.

"Uh, right."

"What was that hood thing you were wearing?" asked Honky.

"It's called a rufter," she explained.

"Could you see out of it?" I asked.

"Not at all," she replied. "Everything was quite dark."

"No doubt conducive to quiet contemplation," noted Norris.

"Er, I suppose," she agreed. "Sometimes they tied leather thongs called jesses to my legs."

"I myself am a believer in self-flagellation," commented Norris.

"Huh?" said our guest.

"And what are the doctrinal tenets of your ecclesiastical order?" inquired Petey.

"The what?"

"Brother Petey, we mustn't ask prying questions," said Norris. "Sister Angelina may have taken a vow of silence on that subject."

"Uh, right," she said. "Say, this champagne is fun."

"It is a soberly nourishing beverage," said Norris, the wine beginning to round off the promontories of his speech. "More cat, sister?"

"Yes, thank you, uh, brother."

"Anyone care for a change of subject?" asked Sunny. "How about incest? I hear it's become a popular leisure-time activity. Shall we discuss that, Bud Brother?"

"I think not," Mr. Gerigar replied.

"May I ask why you are wearing that sock?" inquired Angelina. "Are you cold?"

"I'm not cold," Sunny replied. "It's my Bud honey here who's cold. I'm trying to warm him up by dressing seductively. Have some more champagne, Bud dear."

"I don't mind if I do," he slurred.

"I hope that attack on the mayor was not ill-advised," said Darla.

"I counseled against it," lied Zeb.

"The bastard got what was coming to him," said Norris. "That is to say, his chastisement was divinely ordained."

"I'm glad it happened," said Angelina. "It enabled me to meet all you nice folks."

The large birds exchanged shy smiles.

"I'm still bored," complained Sunny. "How about celibacy as an overrated lifestyle? I hear that topic is a sure-fire ice-breaker at those monastic mixers."

* * *

The morning found us groggy but undebauched. Sister Angelina, who had passed the night on the women's shelf, was impressed that Honky could read the newspaper.

"What is that large black headline?" she asked.

"Just the usual sensationalist twaddle," he replied. "It says: Killer Pigeons Assault Mayor. The article reports the mayor suffered a severe injury to his $2,300 Brioni suit. And they say a valuable falcon was kidnapped."

"How gratifying to know one is valued," said the nun.

"We are all precious in God's eyes," noted Norris.

"Some of us are a bit too precious," added Sunny, now accessorizing her natural peach coloring with a red lace garter, worn looped around her neck. The look was vaguely tropical. "Skip the boring news, Honky. Let's see if Mrs. M's party made the society page."

It did, in spades. There were three large photographs and a write-up peppered with prominent names.

"They're calling it a social triumph," exclaimed Sunny.

"No, they're not," said Honky. "It says right here the party broke up early when a swarm of invading Fubsy Bugs attacked the buffet."

"Hardly a calamity," said Darla. "They were easy enough to pick off."

"And you did it with such delicacy," remarked Zeb.

Believe it or not, she returned his unctuous smile.

We heard a soft crack and a muffled peep. Startled, Julie rose gingerly from her nest, revealing a pink downy mass flopping clumsily amid the remains of the broken egg. It peeped again.

"O-o-oh, it's cute," squealed Blanche.

I exchanged alarmed glances with Petey and Honky. What the hell was a pigeon baby doing in Julie's nest?

* * *

We're in the grip of a moral dilemma. Obviously, at some point—perhaps in the confusion of the flight from the sign or from the park—Phoebe was able to substitute one of her own eggs for Julie's. Clearly the perpetrator of this reprehensible act should be made to account for her treachery. Yet do we have the right to destroy a mother's delight in her new infant, even if said baby is the offspring of another? Which is the greater good?

"It's giving me a headache," whispered Honky, glancing over toward Julie's nest from a remote corner of the attic where we had gathered for a private pow-wow. "I can't make moral decisions without a cigarette and a drink."

"I know how you feel," said Petey. "I say we keep our beaks out of it. As the nipper grows up, Julie will see for herself it's a pigeon."

"But what about Phoebe?" I asked.

"She has her conscience to live with," replied Petey. "She knows she committed a disgraceful act. By the way, in light of these circumstances, I must regretfully decline to marry her."

"Now that's what I call taking a strong ethical stand," I said. "Perhaps you can find some bogus moral reason for rejecting Blanche as well."

"That's not a bad idea," said Petey. "Maybe she was in on the conspiracy."

"I've decided on a name for him," announced the proud new mother from her nest.

Phoebe abruptly withdrew to her trailer and slammed the door.

"What name have you chosen, dear?" asked Darla, mashing Fubsy Bugs for the hungry infant.

"I've decided to call him Honky Junior."

All heads swiveled toward my pale peg-legged pal.

"Honky Junior, huh?" sneered the oafish Yancy. "That don't seem quite right. For one thing, the little bugger's got too many feet."

* * *

Phoebe opened the trailer door and stepped out onto her porch.

"I got an announcement to make," she said. "I'm getting married tomorrow morning to Petey. Everyone's invited except for those who wish me ill."

"Well, that leaves me out," mumbled Petey, looking stunned.

"I also have an announcement," declared Blanche. "*I* am getting married tomorrow morning to Petey. He's not much, but I'm willing to make do. Everyone is invited except for those whose presumption knows no bounds."

The two brides-elect glared at each other; the prospective husband-bigamist stared at them in open-beaked astonishment.

"I have an announcement too," said Sunny. "I'm tying the love knot tomorrow morning with Bud honey. Everyone is invited to bring a tastefully pretentious gift."

"I'm sorry, that is impossible," said Mr. Gerigar. "I can't marry you."

Now it was Sunny's turn to appear stunned. "But why, Bud honey? I'm attractive, I'm affectionate, I'm as sane as modern psychology can make me."

"It's, it's not you," he replied.

"Then what, Bud honey? And besides, what about last night?"

"Sunny, nothing happened last night," he said. "I'm almost sure of it. My objections are not to you—entirely. I've had a unforeseen identity crisis. I've looked into my soul and concluded . . ." The small bird hesitated, obviously distressed.

"Concluded what, dearest one?" Sunny demanded.

"Well, I've concluded that . . ." Again the parakeet hesitated. Everyone gazed at him with rapt attention.

"Spill it," boomed Norris.

"I've concluded I'm a female!"

Stunned silence. Even Honky Junior stopped peeping.

"Don't be ridiculous," said Sunny at last. "That's impossible, Bud honey. You have the worst fashion instincts of any bird I've ever met, not excluding certain unnamed trailer occupants."

"I think she means us, Mom," said baby Ina, adjusting the pink shoelace she had twirled turban-style about her head.

"Nevertheless, I believe I am a female," replied Miss Gerigar. "It's been on my mind for some time now. I've decided to change my name to Verna—an appropriate choice, I think, for someone of my greenish coloration."

"Glad to meet you, Verna," said Kenny.

"Sisters, is it?" sighed Sunny. "I must say, I've wanted many things, but never a sister. Oh, Verna Bud, I knew all that gloomy soul-searching was a mistake. Introspection is the autopsy by the mind of its own entrails. One should never be surprised by the gore."

* * *

All is in an uproar. Phoebe and Blanche each have laid claim to the leftover champagne for tomorrow's festivities. They have also had a nasty spat over a white lace scarf both intend to wear as a wedding gown. Norris and Angelina are praying for a peaceful resolution of this matrimonial crisis. Sunny has retired to her treehouse to nurse her disappointments and spy on Mrs. M. Desperate Petey is talking about emigrating to New Zealand, wherever that is. Jasper and Yancy are sniggering over his misfortunes. Verna is "embracing her maternal nature" by assisting Julie in the nest. I'm trying not to throw up from disgust as Darla receives a prolonged "back rub" from Zeb. Give me a break.

* * *

As dusk descended, the competing wedding preparations were well underway. Both sides are now intriguing to have Brother Norris perform the ceremony.

"What was that noise?" piped Julie, startled.

"It sounded like a loud splash," said Jasper, twitching nervously.

Kenny flew over to the window and peered out. "It's Miguel the gardener," he said. "He's taking a swim in the pool with his wheelbarrow."

I immediately joined the seagull on the window sill. "I don't think Miguel is swimming, Kenny. He's wearing all of his clothes. I think he's in trouble!"

The elderly man flapped and struggled in the deep bath water.

"Norris and Angelina," called Julie, "hurry, you've got to save him!"

"Wait!" protested Zeb. "They can't go out now. It's not dark yet. Someone will see them."

"Oh, Zeb, we can't let him drown!" cried Darla.

"Darla's right," I said. "Norris, Angelina, come with me."

Darting from the window, we swooped down to the pool. The two falcons clamped their great talons onto Miguel's soggy jacket and struggled to pull the floundering man toward the shallow end of the pool. At last he found his footing and staggered—gasping and choking—up the pool steps. The falcons released their grip, and we flew swiftly back to the carriage house.

"Good work," I said to the rescuers. "I don't think anyone saw us."

"Surely someone saw you," said Zeb. "The man you rescued may not see well, but he isn't blind."

We heard a commotion from the garden. A maid had hurried down from the house and was assisting the dripping, half-drowned man, who had begun to shout out words I couldn't understand.

"What's he saying?" asked Darla, alarmed.

"It almost sounds like my name," said the nun.

"Yes, it's Spanish," said Petey. "He's saying: Angels! Angels!"

CHAPTER 22

Along the pool edge: a telltale smear of crushed Fubsy Bugs. My keen detective's eye quickly zeroed in on the cause of Miguel's fall. Indeed, the small furry bugs seem to be growing more numerous by the hour. In the dim garden, now lit only by the pale violet radiance of distant street lamps, the bugs were more felt than seen—as if the entire landscape were aquiver with a ghostly life.

"Damn, I feel like I'm soaking in Fubsy stew," complained Sunny.

"Yes, I think the spa filter's clogged," said Petey. "You can hear the motor laboring."

"It is pleasant though," said Angelina, bouncing slowly up and down in the steaming water.

"You didn't have hot tubs at the convent?" asked Norris.

"Er, no," she replied.

"Your asceticism is to be commended. The mortification of the flesh is much to be desired."

"I'm glad you think something is," she sighed.

"Verna Bud," called Sunny, "did I tell you about the stunning frock Mrs. M was wearing today?"

"Yes, you did, Sunny. Several times in fact."

"Good. We must go window shopping tomorrow along Union Square. The shops are bulging with new spring fashions."

"So you've said, Sunny," she replied. "I suppose I should culti-vate an interest in that field, however frivolous it may seem."

"This hot bath water is very soothing to my stump," said Honky. "Kenny, any chance you could scrounge me up a smoke?"

"Sure, Honky," he replied. "I feel the need for one myself."

The gull climbed out, shook himself off, and flew off toward the street. He didn't get far.

"Hey, everybody," he called from atop the wall, "there's a big crowd of people on the other side!"

Instant alarm.

"Are they cops?" I demanded.

"No, Robin. I don't think so. It's weird. Come see for your-self."

Petey, Zeb, and I followed Kenny to the wall. We alighted on the moss-covered stones and peered cautiously over the edge. Gathered near the wall were dozens of people, each holding a tapered white cylinder surmounted by a flickering flame. Some stood with their eyes closed, mumbling softly to themselves. A few had assumed painful postures on their knees.

"I don't like the looks of this," said Zeb.

"Maybe the cops are sending *people* of prey after us now," I suggested.

We gave a start as something fluttered behind us. Sunny poked her way through and looked down.

"Oh, it's nothing to be concerned about," she said. "It must be Chinese New Years. Francesca always watched the parade and came home with half her clothes singed off from the firecrackers. At least that's what she told her parents."

"But these people don't look Chinese," Petey pointed out.

"Well, neither was Francesca," replied Sunny.

"And I don't hear any firecrackers," said Kenny.

"Maybe we should beat it," said Zeb.

"Don't be silly, Zeb honey," said Sunny. "We've got a great

setup here. You watch, these people will be gone soon. Anyway, I can't desert Mrs. M now. I think she has a new suitor. Either that or she's keeping company with the hunk who reads the gas meter."

* * *

The people have not gone away. They are multiplying like Fubsy Bugs. By the time we returned from our nightly barrel inspection (still empty), the crowd had spilled out into the street, snarling traffic. Shortly thereafter the first ladders hit the wall. We retreated quickly to the attic as invading hordes poured over the stonework and began filling containers of every size and type with dank bath water from the pool.

"Goodness," exclaimed Honky, observing the frenzied scene from the window sill, "there must be some sort of critical bath-water shortage."

Several young men stripped off their clothes and splashed noisily into our once exclusive spa. Other men began clipping branches from the shrubbery and gathering them into neat bundles.

"They must be building nests," speculated Sunny. "Verna Bud, you should study their technique."

"It's getting worse out here," I called back from the window ledge. "Is the trailer packed?"

"Just about, Robin," replied Darla, bustling about in the dark. "Julie's nest is transferred, but Honky Junior is so young to have to move."

"We may not have any choice," I replied.

"I told you we should have cleared out before," complained Zeb. "And, dammit, those falcons should never have rescued that gardener."

"He's right," grunted the brutish Yancy. "It's all their fault."

"Uh-oh, here comes Mrs. M!" called Sunny.

We watched from our attic sanctuary as the lady of the house, clad in a shimmering golden robe, with odd tubular lumps woven into her head feathers, stormed down the path. In one wing she held a long shiny object that projected a brilliant white beam. Accompanying her were her three eldest sons, each carrying a stout wooden stick, which Zeb says are employed in a low sport appropriately termed baseball.

"Get out! Get out!" she shouted, her restless torch flitting over the destructive throngs. "You are all trespassing on private property! Get out!"

Perplexed by the unheeding garden-crashers, Mrs. M swung her light against the skull of the nearest shrubbery-clipper, causing the torch and the trespasser to blink out. Enraged by this defiance of authority, her sons attacked the crowds with their sticks. People screamed, bodies darted in all directions, the half-naked bathers abandoned the spa, panicked bottle-fillers clambered back over the wall. Baseball sticks swung against air, against trees, against people. Then the scene was illuminated by a vastly brighter beam, and from overhead we heard the menacing wing-beat of its source: the police helicopter.

"Oh, no! It's the cops!" twitched Jasper.

From all directions came the wails of approaching sirens.

"Let's go!" I shouted. "Now! We haven't a moment to lose!"

"Robin!" cried Darla. "Julie's baby! He's missing!"

* * *

Separated in the tumult from his presumed mother, Honky Junior had sought refuge under Sunny's wardrobe pile. After a desperate fifteen-minute search, the lost infant was discovered, but by then the grounds were swarming with blue-uniformed officers. The helicopter had retired, but now a massed radiance brighter than the sun was shining down on the garden from what Zeb identified as a row of television news trucks positioned on the other side of the wall. Telescoped up from the roof of each truck were tall metal poles, tipped by glaring lights and saucer-like dishes aimed toward the heavens.

"We're trapped," said Zeb. "If we try to escape now, the cops will shoot us for sure."

"It's only a matter of time before they come up here," added Jasper, his twitch taking on a convulsive new urgency.

"It'd take a miracle for us to get out of here alive," whined Yancy.

"Then why not give them a miracle," calmly suggested Sister Angelina. "After all, that's what these people have come to see."

"Are you thinking what I'm thinking, Sister?" I asked.

"I hope so, Brother Robin," she replied.

* * *

"OK, everyone," I said, "now remember to stay in formation. It's important that we keep as close together as possible. And try not to get tangled up in each other's equipment."

"Are you sure this will work?" demanded Blanche.

"It's our only chance," I replied. "OK, we lift off at the count of three. One. Two. *Three!*"

Fluttering en masse, we rose into the air, lurched from side to side, and sailed uncertainly out through the broken attic window. Trailing scarves and handkerchiefs, Kenny and I took the lead. Behind us, bedecked in silken lingerie, came Norris and Angelina towing the trailer, draped in a lacy white slip. More scarves and ribbons streamed from the balance of our troupe, tightly massed around the disguised mobile home containing Julie and the youngsters.

Almost immediately the television lights converged upon us, as murmurs of astonishment went through the great crowd.

"Oh my God!" I heard Mrs. M exclaim.

Rumbles of wonder rippled through the throngs as we rose higher and higher into the starless black sky.

"Don't shoot, men!" we heard a man shout.

"It's a miracle!" someone cried.

"The angel! The angel!" voices sang out. "The angel! The angel!"

"Stay together!" I commanded.

"Verna Bud," called Sunny. "It's our first fashion show. And we're a hit!"

"Look out, Robin!" shouted Kenny. "Here comes the police helicopter!"

Flashing red lights and whirling blades bore down on us out of the night with frightening speed.

"Oh, Robin!" called Darla. "What should we do?"

"If they start firing, everyone disperse," I replied, my right eye fixed on the fast-approaching mechanical monster, my left eye trained on the two falcons and their burden. "Try to make a run for it. Kenny and I will attack the pilot."

Then an immense wave of sound rose from the crowd. "No! No!" they cried. The swelling roar rolled up and buffeted us like a sudden wind. "No! No!"

"It's turning!" shouted Kenny.

It was true. The helicopter veered away. A thunderous cheer rose from the crowd.

We were safe.

We flew west to the sounds of distant foghorns. Across the city, the twin flood-lit towers of the great bridge rose above the fog like orange beacons in the night.

CHAPTER 23

"Experts are examining the TV news videos," said Honky, reading the morning paper. "They think the alleged Angel of Pacific Heights may be Killer Pigeons in disguise."

"Save us from the professional skeptics," said Norris.

"Did we commit a great wrong by misleading those people?" asked Angelina.

"Not at all," I replied. "People came to witness a miracle and they did. They saw a band of defenseless refugees escape from a large force of heavily armed police."

"I hope we're safe here," said Darla, gazing up warily. "Those sad ladies make me feel so self-conscious."

Today's shelter was identified by Petey as a large concrete box atop a peristyle of grand Corinthian columns. The temple-like structure beneath us rose like a vision of ancient Greece beside a serene, Fubsy Bug-infested lagoon. At the center of the peristyle, etched in ethereal pinks against the olive hills of the Presidio, was a great domed rotunda—its coffered and frescoed interior mirrored in the still waters of the lagoon.

At each exterior corner of our lofty box stood a scantily clad stone woman, resting her weathered arms on the top edge and peering down in doleful perplexity at the inner void—now occupied by our bedraggled troupe and Phoebe's well-traveled trailer. Above the ornate architrave of the curving colonnade, dozens more stone women draped themselves in identical postures of woe on similar concrete boxes.

"What is this place?" asked Blanche. "It gives me the creeps."

"Don't you remember?" said Julie. "It was depicted on that pennant in the carriage house. It must be from the Panama-Pacific International Exposition."

"You sound like tourists," said Sunny. "It's the Palace of Fine Arts. Everyone knows that."

"What is its function?" asked Julie.

"It's art," Sunny replied. "Its function is to be beautiful."

"But it's so big!" exclaimed Blanche. "It must have cost a fortune."

"Yes, people used to devote money to art," explained Miss Gerigar. "They don't any more. It's not a cost-effective use of public resources."

"Well, it's a pretty spot for a wedding," said Phoebe, opening her trailer window. I noticed she was dressed in white lace.

"Honky, the newspaper can wait," said Petey, suddenly rousing himself. "We must engage in serious detective work. That missing mannequin maker must be found."

I agreed. "Yes, vital scouting must be performed without delay. Let's go men."

For once I didn't have to ask them twice.

* * *

We began our intelligence-gathering expedition by sharing a smoke in the park across the street from Mrs. M's besieged mansion. If anything, the festive crowd was even larger than when we had departed. TV trucks now circled the estate, and mounds of flowers—some in elaborately wrought arrangements—threatened to engulf the garden wall. Mrs. M was nowhere to be seen, but several of her younger offspring were observed heaving what Petey identified as water balloons from a second-floor window at TV news people.

"I hope we didn't excessively inconvenience Mrs. M," said Honky, bogarting the smoke.

"Of course we didn't," I assured him. "All these people constitute a tremendous fund-raising opportunity for her. She's probably overseeing the hors d'oeuvres preparation as we speak. That reminds me, Honky, you are seriously bogarting our cigarette."

"Aw, Kenny's bringing some more," he replied, continuing to puff away. Honky's accident had removed more than his foot. It had also excised our pal's last weak impulse to share.

"Robin, do you see Mr. Trinello?" asked Honky.

"Of course not. I don't know what the man looks like. I've only seen him with pantyhose over his head."

"Then how are we supposed to find him?" he asked.

"Easy," I replied. "We merely have to stake out an area with a large concentration of artificial people."

"That won't be so easy," said Petey. "Los Angeles is over 450 miles away."

"Petey, I was referring to Union Square."

"Oh, good," he said, "maybe the Pigeon Chow Lady is out of jail."

* * *

She was. While Kenny stood watch in a nearby palm tree for cops with nets, we flew down to her well-stocked bosom eatery.

"Ah, my precious friends!" she exclaimed, sprinkling on an extra-generous wingful. "You've chosen an excellent time to visit. The Square is practically deserted. Those pleasant Fubsy Bugs have driven away most of the tourists. My, you *have* been busy. I was so proud of the way you outsmarted the police on their outrageous birds-of-prey ploy. I think training birds to attack their fellow creatures is simply criminal. Leave it to the police to hatch such a wicked scheme. Be assured, my dears, you are not alone. You have friends, many friends—some of them in very high places. The outrage is mounting. Yes, you have been treated abominably."

"You can say that again," said Petey, gulping sunflower seeds with his usual dispatch.

Our benefactress looked around warily and lowered her voice. "I have heard through my sources that the murder accusation against you was a trumped-up charge. I don't mind telling you I was relieved. Candidly, I must confess I was briefly shaken, but one can lose one's perspective while imprisoned. Yes, I was in jail. I don't suppose you knew about that. Then I heard from Ted about his missing inventory and we put two and two together. Ted is your friend too. He and his associates are doing wonderful work. They're planning another glorious liberation tonight. Right here in the city—at UC Medical Center. I wish I could go with them, but I am too well-known to the police. Ted says taking me along would be like waving a red flag at a bull. And we all know who the bull is. My, you have good appetites. I'm glad to see you're getting enough to eat."

She sprinkled on another big wingful. "Dine on, my angels. Angels! Ha-ha, I must remember to tell that to Ted if he comes by again. He's over at Macy's today updating some facial expressions. Aloof disdain is no longer in, he informs me. Ted does wonderful work, though, of course, there is a great deal of sexism and fat oppression in his art. But like most of us he is a slave to commercial reality. Fortunately, a small family trust fund liberated me from the iron grip of trade. Father invented a terribly effective gopher trap, and I am spending his fortune as best I can to make amends. I am trying to persuade Ted to introduce gophers into Union Square. Wouldn't that be wonderful? All those lovely little mounds of soil here and there as evidence of their indomitable underground enterprise."

"What is that woman talking about?" asked Honky.

"Something about subway construction, I think," said Petey. "And who is this Ted person?"

"It's Mr. Trinello, of course," I replied. "It must be. This has been an extremely informative conversation."

"And an extremely filling alternative to holy wedlock," belched Petey.

* * *

Within 20 minutes Kenny had spotted the dented white van parked in an alley not far from Darla's favorite dumpster. I hoped she would not be visiting it soon in the company of a tot-mugging gigolo. As the rear van doors were open, the three of us flew into the back and quickly concealed ourselves inside mannequin legs. Only Kenny, under orders to follow the van by air, remained outside. He flew up to a window ledge, and we all settled in to wait for Ted Trinello's return.

"I wish I had a cigarette," said Petey from a neighboring leg.

"A tote of sherry would be nice too," I heard Honky reply.

With a startling crash the rear doors suddenly swung closed. A moment later the front door opened, and the seat sagged and creaked as a burly figure entered. Through the round knee joint of my mannequin hiding place, I could see a section of flabby, plaid-shirted torso protruding above a broad, khaki-covered haunch. The man's well-muscled featherless wingtip reached up and turned a shiny metal implement, activating a familiar mechanical rumbling. It was the same rhythmic pulsations we had heard the night of our abduction!

Ted Trinello (for I knew our driver was the roguish ARF leader himself) then pulled down a small lever and pressed his dusty right boot against a floor-mounted mechanism. Immediately, the van began to move. Whistling a cheerful tune, he turned a large spoked wheel back and forth, apparently controlling the van's direction of movement.

"Flying is OK," whispered Honky, "but I'd love to have my own car."

"Too much bother," I replied. "Mr. Spade always takes taxis.

Or you can do like Sunny and cadge free rides on the roofs of streetcars."

"I know," he whispered, "but it's not the same."

After innumerable starts, stops, turns, and nausea-inducing swerves, the van at last came to rest. The man returned the lever to its uppermost position and switched back the metal implement, silencing the rumbling. He quickly exited without rolling up his window or locking the door.

"Robin," called Honky, "where do you suppose we are?"

"From the sounds of seagulls in the distance, I'd say we must be near the bath-water bay."

Kenny flew in through the window and hopped down onto the recently vacated seat.

"You're in a waterfront district well south of the Bay Bridge," he reported. "The suspect just entered a derelict metal building which may function as a mannequin repair facility."

"What makes you say that, Kenny?" I asked.

"I looked in through a window, Robin. He's got body parts strewn from one end to another."

"Any blood?" I asked.

"Not that I can see."

"OK, we can tentatively rule out mass murder. They're probably mannequins. Good work, Kenny."

"What now, Robin?" he asked.

"You keep watch outside, Kenny. We'll remain here on stake-out duty. What is your impression of the suspect?"

"Well offhand, I'd say the guy has an extremely productive halibut source."

* * *

Hours and hours and hours have gone by. Not even a magazine to read. Of course, everyone is desperate for a cigarette, but we don't dare sneak one into the van. No stray butts under the seats either, although we did find something that looks suspiciously like women's black fishnet pantyhose. Thank goodness we had had a proper lunch. At least hunger is not exacerbating our numerous bodily cravings. I wonder what Sam Spade does on boring stakeouts? He probably has the foresight to bring along a bottle. I imagine he settles back, lights a cigarette, thinks of absent Brigid, and gets quietly smashed—all on the client's tab.

To pass the time we have resorted to that universal diversion: gossip.

"I may be holed up in a cramped mannequin leg," remarked Petey, "but at least I'm missing my wedding."

"I don't think Phoebe minds that much," said Honky.

"Doesn't mind?" blustered Petey. "Of course she minds. I'm breaking her poor heart, dammit."

"No, you're not," he replied. "She doesn't want to marry you."

"She doesn't!" Petey exclaimed. "Then why did she make that wedding announcement? And dress up in all that silly lace?"

Honky lowered his voice. "I heard Julie tell Darla that Phoebe's just trying to make someone jealous."

"Who?" Petey demanded.

"It's Yancy. The word is Phoebe's been stuck on him ever since he showed up with his two buddies."

"That's perfect," I said. "Yancy would make an ideal mate for Phoebe."

"I couldn't agree more," said Petey. "And it wouldn't surprise me if Blanche has her sights trained on ol' Jasper. That could explain the fellow's chronic jumpiness."

"Nah, you're wrong there, Petey," said Honky. "I got the scoop on that too. I heard her tell Julie that she couldn't stand you personally, but has always deeply loved you."

"I feel the same way about her," said Petey. "Except for the love part."

* * *

Hours after nightfall. We're finally on the move. The nefarious Ted Trinello, now dressed completely in black, has picked up a passenger, whose scent and voice I recognized from the lab. It's the woman whose wing I nearly amputated—the homicidal kidnapper who once demanded that Ted shoot me.

"Are we picking up the others?" she asked.

"No, they're meeting us there in Rupert's car. He's got the passkey."

"I don't know about this, Ted. There's still a lot of heat coming down from the pigeon job."

"I know, Jessie. But this can't wait. According to Rupert's informant, tomorrow they start sticking electrodes into the brains of those cats."

"We've got to save them, Ted," she said.

"Goodness," whispered Honky. "They're going to liberate cats!"

"I knew we were dealing with master criminals," I replied, "but I never imagined they would stoop to such depravity."

* * *

Many miles later. I felt the van turn left, roll over two bumps, then back slowly down a slope. It came to a stop, Ted switched off the rumbling, and he and his black-garbed Mata Hari quickly exited. We heard other muted voices behind the van, then a door somewhere opened and closed. Right then Kenny flew in through the window.

"You're at some kind of loading dock," he reported. "They've put pantyhose over their heads and gone into the building. Some of them have guns."

"Good work, Kenny," I said. "How far are we from the Palace of Fine Arts?"

"Not far, Robin. It's just across the park and down the hill."

"Good. I want you to go there, Kenny. As fast as possible. Bring back the others. We'll need Wally Junior and baby Ina too. But tell Darla to stay behind with Julie and the baby."

"Will do," said the seagull, flying off.

"Robin, what do we do now?" asked Honky.

"Just lay low until I give the word."

"I hope those damn cats are in cages," muttered Petey.

They were. Several minutes later, black-garbed figures began loading metal cages of cats into the back of the van. Cage after cage of yowling, shrieking, hissing cats. More cats—of all sizes and colors—than I ever imagined existed. And still the cages kept coming, until the van was loaded nearly to the ceiling.

"Holy shit!" muttered Petey. "It's a catastro . . . I mean a disaster."

From behind the mountain of cats a man's voice grunted, "That's it, Ted. She's full up."

"Damn. OK, we'll take the rest in Rupert's car."

"But there's not enough room," the man objected.

"I can see that," snapped Ted. "We'll carry them without the cages."

"Are you sure that's a good idea, Ted?" asked a voice that sounded like Jessie's. "These sweet kitties are pretty shook up."

"We'll manage," Ted replied, as the rear van doors slammed closed. "Help me carry this last load over."

A moment later Kenny and Zeb fluttered in through the window.

"Good work, Kenny," I said, emerging from the leg. "I want everybody in here immediately."

"But this is insanity!" protested Zeb. "This vehicle is full of cats."

"What a treasure trove!" exclaimed Norris, flying in through the other open window. "You hit the jackpot, Robin. We eat for months. It's just like Christmas morning!"

The cats, I noticed, had suddenly grown very quiet.

CHAPTER 24

"Where are the parakeets?" I asked, darting up to the very top of the driver's seat.

"Sunny and Verna had a small emergency," replied Sister Angelina, quickly taking her assigned position beside Norris on the floor.

"Your Mr. Gerigar laid an egg," cackled Yancy from his perch next to his fellow tot-muggers and Petey on the left spoke of the steering-wheel.

"Fatherhood came as a great shock to Sunny," added Blanche, lining up on the right spoke next to Phoebe and her children. "That will teach the reckless bird to guzzle champagne while masquerading as a female."

"Quick, Robin!" called Honky from his observation post on the paper-cluttered windshield ledge. "They're coming!"

"OK, Kenny," I commanded. "Switch it."

The seagull turned the shiny metal implement; a loud grinding noise was heard and the mechanical rumbling commenced. Across the parking lot, Ted shouted something to his gang; they dropped the cages, and ran toward us.

"OK, Kenny," I called, "the lever!"

The seagull hopped up on the lever, pushing it down with his weight. The van lurched forward; I nearly toppled backwards off the seat.

"OK, Norris," I shouted. "Jump on it!"

The falcon applied his considerable weight to the pedal-like implement on the floor. Immediately, the rumbling intensified and the van shot forward at frightening speed—heading straight toward the gesticulating ARF raiders. I hoped they would get out of the way in time. They did—just barely. We bounced over several unseen impediments, possibly a sign post and concrete curb, and hurtled onward.

"OK, right group!" I shouted. "Right group!"

As instructed, the right-side occupants gripped the spoke and fluttered their wings, thus turning the wheel (and the van) to the left. As I had hoped, we bounced back down over the curb and into what felt like the road.

"OK, left group. Just a little. Steady. Now, right group. Damn, it's pitch black. I can barely see where I'm going."

"Allow me," said Kenny, pulling out a knob near the metal activation implement. Suddenly, the road ahead of us was ablaze with light, enabling me to see the large building looming directly in our path.

"Angelina! Angelina!" I shouted. The falcon nun dutifully applied her lever as Norris let up on his. "Left group! Left group!" The van slowed, swerved to the right, and narrowly missed the building. Up ahead cars streamed back and forth on a broad, busy street.

"Uh-oh!" shouted Honky, peering into the rear-view mirror. "They're following us in Rupert's car!"

"Good," I said, praying for an interruption in the heavy cross-traffic ahead. "Norris, step on it!"

"Look out!" shouted Kenny. Like a crazed woodpecker, the panicked seagull dashed his head against the center of the steering wheel, producing loud blasts of noise. The van darted boldly through a fortuitous gap in the traffic as cars swerved and lurched around us—some, I noticed, crashing loudly into their neighbors.

Right behind us came our speeding pursuers.

"Angelina! Right group! Right group! OK, steady it. Norris!"

We accelerated down the busy street, identified by ever-watchful Honky as Lincoln Way. Kenny continued to bash his head against the horn as I endeavored to steer us straight down the yellow guidance line conveniently placed in the middle of the highway. Most drivers, perhaps recognizing my status as a neophyte, managed to dodge out of the way, although I was forced to direct glancing, metal-crunching blows against several obdurate road-hoggers.

"Honky," I called, "are they still following us?"

"Yeah, Robin. But it looks like Ted's having trouble driving. The whole car's crawling with scared cats. Oops, one just jumped on his head."

"Police car dead ahead!" screamed Kenny.

"Angelina! Left group! Left group! Norris!"

We skidded through a high-speed right turn and pressed on, followed by the cat-abductors and wailing police car. Somehow we had passed instantly from city to countryside.

"Right group. Steady. Left group. Good, steady. Kenny, what is this place?"

"Golden Gate Park, Robin."

"At least the traffic's lighter. OK, right group. Steady."

"Police car blocking road ahead!" shouted Honky.

"Damn! Angelina! Left group! Left group! Norris!"

Another hairpin right turn put us on a narrow road circling a bath-water lake shimmering silver in the moonlight. Parked along the road were a series of darkened cars, their windows mysteriously steamed up. We inadvertently sideswiped several, as did Ted and the legion of pursuing police cars.

Having completed a hasty tour of the lake district, I directed our battered, smoking van down another road, which fed into a broader, less demandingly sinuous avenue.

"Right group. Steady. Norris. Steady. Kenny, where are we now?"

"Uh, JFK Drive, I think. It leads out of the park."

"Good. Steady. Norris."

"Major law enforcement roadblock ahead!" cried Honky.

"No problemo," I said, feeling new confidence in my rapidly maturing driving skills. "Angelina! Left group! Left group! Norris!"

"Uh-oh," gasped Kenny.

Instant panic. "What's wrong?" I demanded.

"Robin, this is a cul-de-sac."

"Hey, speak my language!"

"It's a dead-end road."

"Damn!"

"Stop ahead!" shouted my one-legged co-pilot.

"Angelina! Angelina! Oh, what the hell. Norris!"

The road ended, we hit the curb, and were suddenly airborne. As if we could fly. Hey, we can fly. The van soared upward, the wheel grippers deserted their posts, I braced for impact, ten thousand cats broke into deafening lamentations. Through the windshield I saw an elegant white structure topped by a glittering dome. It was flying toward us at great speed. It overtook us. We crashed through its fragile glass skin, spun around, and lurched to a stop in a dim humid jungle, dense with strange, unearthly plantlife.

"Abandon ship!" I shouted, picking myself up from where I knew not. "Let's get out of here!"

* * *

"I can't believe we escaped without a single cat," said Norris."

"Well, Brother Norris, they were all in cages," said Sister Angelina. "We should be thankful that no one was seriously injured. How is your wing?"

"Bunged up, Sister," the falcon replied. "It feels pretty stiff this morning, but that is God's will."

"Amen, Brother," she replied. "Shall I rub it?"

"Please do."

Our second morning in the austerely palatial concrete box found Petey and me sharing our first smoke of the day as Honky puffed his own personal Stalem and avidly scanned the newspaper.

"What's the headline?" asked Miss Gerigar from her modest, newly constructed nest atop the trailer sundeck.

"Suspects Nabbed as Killer Pigeons Betray ARF Raiders," read Honky. "There's also a sidebar: Runaway Van Damages Conservatory of Flowers."

"It wasn't a runaway," Wally Junior pointed out. "Uncle Robin and the rest of us were driving. We had it perfectly under control."

"It was tons of fun," added baby Ina. "Can we steal another car today, Uncle Robin?"

"I don't think so," I replied, glancing warily at the strangely quiet Darla.

"It says here the D.A. will be throwing the book at Ted and his gang," added Honky. "They are expected to be charged with more than a dozen major felonies."

"Good," I said. "That should put them away for a nice long time."

"I expect it will," said Darla.

"You don't sound very happy about it," said Petey.

"I don't know," she sighed. "As you yourself pointed out, Robin, they're all good friends of the Pigeon Chow Lady, who, it seems to me, has always had our best interests at heart."

"They were plotting to release cats," I pointed out, "hundreds of them."

"I know, Robin," she replied. "And that doesn't seem right."

"I was opposed to the whole mad scheme," said Zeb, patting her on the back.

Sunny circled down from one of the doleful stone ladies.

"How's Mrs. M?" asked Julie, feeding a mashed Fubsy Bug to her chirping infant.

"Didn't see the dame," replied the parakeet, walking about on the trailer roof in his approximation of a swagger. "But that herd of posey-toting galoots is still camped out around her house. How's the egg, Verna?"

"About the same," his mate replied.

"Sunny, I'm sorry I misled you about your sex," I said.

The parakeet hoisted himself up to his full eleven-centimeter height. "I'll be settling your hash later," he said. "Or should I say, scrambling your brains."

"It's not Robin's fault," protested Miss Gerigar. "Sunny, you're the victim of serious professional malpractice. I don't know how to make it up to you."

"Just keep looking gorgeous, babe," he winked. "I'll think of something."

* * *

The oft-delayed wedding has been rescheduled (by Phoebe) for sunset tonight. To Petey's distress, Yancy received the news with either artfully simulated or sincerely genuine indifference. To circumvent Darla's ban and divert suspicion, we sent Sister Angelina into a Marina District liquor store for an emergency bottle to fortify the groom. The brazen tot-muggers crashed our afternoon bachelors' party, held in what Petey identified as an abandoned gun emplacement dug into the overgrown cliffs high above the Golden Gate.

"Great tactical position," commented Sunny, sighting down the old concrete gun mounts. "Be just like shooting ducks in a barrel. Hell, if I had a rifle with a high-powered scope, I'd pick me off a couple of those damn windsurfers right now."

"Why would you want to do that?" inquired Kenny.

Sunny expectorated. He was wearing Mrs. M's old red leather watchband as a bandoleer across his chest. "For the sport of it, I reckon. Why else? Say, want to wrestle?"

"Not with you," sneered the gull.

"These fried pork rinds are excellent," said Norris. "Sister Angelina, we must track down and eat a pig."

"Good idea, Brother Norris. We could build an altar and offer it up in an inspiring, albeit bloody ritual."

"An animal sacrifice," said Norris. "What a splendid idea."

"So, Petey," said Zeb, bogarting the sherry, "you're finally tying the old knot."

"I suppose so," he sighed.

"Of course," continued Zeb, "there's a way out—if you'd rather not."

"I know," Petey said listlessly. "Throw myself off this cliff. I should have done it back before I learned to fly."

"No, I mean you could return to the lab," said Zeb.

"We wish," I said. "No one knows how to get back to the lab."

"That's not exactly true," said Zeb.

"What do you mean?" I demanded.

"Yeah, Zeb," said Yancy. "Spill it."

"Darla knows where the lab is," Zeb replied. "She told me so yesterday."

"I'm saved!" cried Petey. "Zeb, pass me that bottle quick."

* * *

"Zebulon, you betrayed a private confidence," said Darla, angrily stuffing an unmashed Fubsy Bug down Honky Junior's tiny throat. He didn't seem to mind.

"Sorry, Darla dearest," Zeb replied, "it slipped out."

"Can you take us back to the lab?" demanded Yancy.

"Oh, I don't know. I suppose," she replied. "But it's a long way and over water too. The distance might be too much for you smokers."

"But, Darla, you said there was a bridge," Zeb pointed out. "They could rest on the bridge if they get tired."

"The Golden Gate Bridge?" I asked.

"No, the Bay Bridge," she replied. "Oh, Robin, you don't want to go back do you?"

"We have to go, Darla. We owe it to Dr. Milbrene. But anyone who doesn't wish to go is welcome to stay behind."

"I'm staying," declared Blanche. "I suppose, Petey, you'll be abandoning us?"

"With great reluctance, my dear."

"Bullbleep," she retorted.

Her white lace in disarray, Phoebe dashed out of the trailer and threw her wings around Yancy. "Oh my darling!" she sobbed. "Don't leave me!"

"Will somebody please get this hysterical pigeon off my neck?" he said, recoiling.

"I also must stay," announced Julie. "I have my son to take care of. I don't want him to grow up in a cage. Are you going, Honky dear?"

"Yes, I must," he replied. "But maybe we'll all come back after Dr. Milbrene concludes his experiments."

"I'm going with you too," vowed the seagull.

"No, Kenny," I said. "You have to stay here and help take care of our friends. Zeb, are you coming?"

"Certainly not. And neither is Jasper."

The skinny tot-mugger twitched in agreement.

"Robin, I must counsel against this course of action," said Miss Gerigar from her nest.

"A careful man may cage his dreams," added Sunny. "But only a fool dreams of cages."

"I'm sorry," I replied. "My mind is made up. We leave to-night."

CHAPTER 25

We flew east through thick grey fog. I wondered if we had the strength for such a long journey: all the way across the city, then along the span of the great bridge, and then who knows how far beyond that? Once I had conceived of the world as a realm no larger than ten times the size of our laboratory home. Who could have imagined that beyond those familiar walls lay such a frightening immensity of space?

"Darla, let's not fly so high," called Honky, lagging behind in the swirling darkness.

"We're not astronauts," gasped Petey. "We don't have to attempt a lunar orbit."

"Oh, all right," grumbled Darla, banking left and gliding lower over the fringe of downtown. "But try not to crash into any trees."

"Hey, there's Effie's building," Honky pointed out.

"Be prepared to dodge some bullets," panted Petey.

I glanced down and noticed a lone figure pause in a doorway and casually light a cigarette. It was a tall man in a dark suit. His head turned as he blew out the match, and from under the brim of his hat yellow-grey horizontal eyes gazed up at me. A passing car briefly illuminated his long, bony jaw. The man turned and strode briskly down the sidewalk.

"My, my God," I stammered, almost falling out of the sky. "It's him!"

"It's who?" inquired Petey.

"It's him! It's Mr. Spade!"

"Where?" exclaimed Honky.

"Down there!" I shouted. "Follow me!"

I catapulted into the steepest dive of my life. Up ahead the man glanced back, turned to the right, and walked into the deep shadows between two buildings.

"Robin!" called Darla from far overhead. "Wait up!"

"What's the rush?" complained Zeb, who had volunteered to come along as Darla's escort.

I glided down between the buildings and landed in the fetid dampness of a narrow alley. Dim bare bulbs over shuttered doors stabbed crazy shadows across the high brick walls. Cold bath water fell in solitary drops from distant roofs; a chill wind stirred the leaden fog and scattered the litter in the gutter.

"Where is he?" asked Petey, landing heavily behind me.

I glanced desperately left and right as my companions fluttered down around me.

"Which way did he go?" asked Honky.

"I don't see anyone," said Zeb.

"Yeah, me neither," grunted Yancy. "What's goin' on?"

"Robin, there's no one here," said Darla.

"He must be here!" I shouted. "I saw him come this way."

I listened intently. No footsteps. The alley was deserted.

"Oh, Robin, look," said Darla, pointing.

We all turned.

On the wall of a building: the dull sheen of metal.

"It's some sort of plaque," I said. "Honky, what does it say?"

Honky studied the raised letters just visible in the dim light of a far-away street lamp. "I don't believe it," he gasped.

"What is it?" demanded Petey.

Honky looked at me, then turned back toward the sign. "It says: On approximately this spot Miles Archer, partner of Sam

Spade, was done in by Brigid O'Shaughnessy."

"Brigid shot Miles!" exclaimed Petey.

"That's impossible," I said, stunned. "Floyd Thursby shot Miles. And then someone—probably Joel Cairo—iced Thursby."

"But, Robin, why does this sign implicate Brigid?" asked Darla.

"It does more than implicate her," Zeb pointed out.

"I have no idea," I replied. "Mr. Spade could never fall in love with a woman who killed his partner. He's much too savvy for that."

"Yes, well sometimes people are not exactly what they seem," said Darla. "And even intelligent people can be duped."

"Meaning what?" I demanded.

"Robin, Dr. Milbrene and Maryanne may . . . they may not have our best interests at heart."

"Maryanne's a doll," said Yancy. "She wouldn't hurt a feather on my handsome head."

"And Dr. Milbrene is practically a Nobel laureate," I pointed out. "No, Darla, your suspicions are sadly misplaced. It's late. Shall we go?"

"All right, Robin," she sighed. "Whatever you say."

* * *

Darla was right about one thing. The journey to Berkeley was long and difficult. Flying directly toward the rising sun, we puffed from tower to tower on the great silver bridge, then worked our way across grim industrial districts toward the beckoning campus (identified by Darla) gleaming white on a distant hill. By the time we arrived at last on a ledge outside a window of our lab the day was almost over. Far below us, the fading sun was flinging its pink-tinged radiance across the bath-water bay and hanging golden tinsel on lavender clouds suspended beneath a coral sky.

"Well, this is it," said Darla softly.

"Yes, it has an air of familiarity about it," observed Petey with ill-concealed excitement.

"Zeb, are you sure you don't want to come in with us?" I asked.

"Not on your life," he replied.

"Robin, I'm not coming in either," said Darla.

"But, Darla, why not?" I asked.

"There's nothing in there for me, Robin. And besides, the others need me."

"Darla, I don't know what to say . . ."

"Give our regards to the others," said Honky.

"Yes, please do," added Petey.

"Would you like us to hang around out here for a while?" asked Darla. "In case there's trouble?"

"No, that won't be necessary," I said. "We'll be fine. Thanks for everything, Darla."

"I, I hope it works out for you, Robin," she said. "I'll miss you."

"And I'll miss you too," I said. "All of you."

"Darla, it'll be dark soon," said Zeb impatiently. "We should go."

"I see Maryanne!" exclaimed Yancy, tapping frantically on the glass. "She's coming this way!"

I turned around and peered eagerly in through the window as behind me Darla and Zeb fluttered away. A pale featherless wingtip released the latch, the window opened, and I inhaled the sweet familiar scent of my love. She looked out and smiled, melting my inner ice caps and swamping my heart with tidal waves of joy.

"Dr. Milbrene!" she called. "They're back!"

"What's that strange odor?" whispered Honky.

"Cat," replied Petey. "It smells like cat."

* * *

The lab has been taken over by cats. Cage after cage of hairy smelly cats, puffing on our Drag-O-Matics, sucking on our sherry tubes, and crunching noisily on Yancy's fried pork rinds. It's all very unsettling. And why did dear Maryanne put us in a Control

Group cage? Just a tray of oddly stale Hygienic Pigeon Chow, but no vital Drag-O-Matic or essential sherry tube.

"I'm dying for a cigarette," said Honky. "All these cats are making me extremely nervous."

"I need a drink," said Petey. "Now."

"I expect Maryanne went to fill some sherry tubes with champagne," I said. "A special occasion like this calls for a real celebration."

"Maybe they'll give us each our own cigar," suggested Honky.

"That babe is looking choice," grunted Yancy. "Really choice."

At that moment the object of Yancy's base lust emerged with Dr. Milbrene from his office. The eminent biologist was not smiling.

"So, the prodigal Killer Pigeons have returned, have they?"

"It's them, Dr. Milbrene," said Maryanne excitedly. "See, Honky has the gold peg on his missing leg."

"And where's the rest of your gang?" he demanded. "Still out there sowing havoc, assaulting government officials, and compounding my legal woes?"

"The guy looks pissed," whispered Yancy.

"What shall I do with them, Dr. Milbrene?" asked Maryanne.

"Process them, of course."

"But, Dr. Milbrene," she objected, "the tests are corrupted. The data would be meaningless."

"I'll decide issues of relevance, Maryanne. As far as I'm concerned the test animals all returned, we processed them promptly, and moved on to a new round of tests with a different species, namely felines. That's what the documentation will show. You process these animals tonight. But leave the date blank for me to fill in."

"But, Dr. Milbrene. . ."

"I want the data on my desk tomorrow," he insisted. "I've had it. I never want to see another damn pigeon!"

A collective gasp in our cage.

"Dr. Milbrene called us pigeons!" exclaimed Honky.

My head swirled, my brain reeled. My self-image staggered back and forth, teetered on the brink, and toppled into an abyss of confusion.

"What's 'process' mean?" asked Yancy, seemingly unperturbed by this lightning-quick identity shift.

"I think they're going to check our temperature," said Petey. "You know, give us a physical exam."

"My temperature is hot," bragged Yancy. "Hot for Maryanne!"

* * *

One nervous hour later. Having refilled all of the lab's Drag-O-Matics, Maryanne wiped her hands on a towel and walked over to our cage.

"Sorry, boys," she said, opening the door. "Which one wants to go first?"

"I'll go," I said, sensing a darker purpose behind Dr. Milbrene's ambiguous word.

"Forget it, Robin," said Yancy, hopping up onto her hand. "You never had a chance with this babe. She's mine!"

Maryanne closed and latched the cage, and—softly stroking Yancy's head—carried the leering tot-mugger into the adjoining equipment room. He glanced back at me in smug satisfaction.

His triumph was shortlived.

I will spare you the grisly details—the ominous clatter of instruments, the sudden shrieking abruptly terminated by a shocking thwack, the plucking of feathers, the rending of flesh, the crunching of bone, the plonk against the stainless steel counter of quivering, gouged-out organs, the whirl of grinders, the high-pitched wail of the liver-digesting centrifuge, the final sickening sprong of the waste container lid as the plundered cadaver was rudely discarded.

Yes, my love is a murderer, as was—I now have no doubt—Brigid O'Shaughnessy. Sam Spade himself had sent me a sign, and I foolishly ignored it. Darla was right, just as she was almost always right. Both the great San Francisco detective and I had been deceived—taken in by a woman's coy smile. The toll for him (I assume) was loneliness and heartbreak; I was to pay for my folly with my life. And worse, the lives of my friends.

Maryanne returned, wiping her foul hands on the same besmirched towel.

"I never cared much for that bird," she remarked.

"Yes, he may have sensed that at the end," gasped Petey.

The murderess approached our cage and unclicked the latch. I felt the icy grip of terror, my heart pounded wildly in my breast; I gazed one last time at my loyal companions. I made the only decision possible: I would be the next one to go.

Maryanne paused. "Oh, I've got all night," she said, re-clicking the latch. "I have all those cages to clean. Cats are much more work than you fellows were. Now I don't even have time to read."

* * *

OK, I'm not a person, I'm a pigeon. I'm a sawed-off urban bird with identity problems. Like Norris, I clung to my illusions rather than face the inappropriateness of my love. He gave his heart to a metal statuette; I entrusted mine to a homicidal human. I lived in a chimerical world of romantic delusion. So sweet was the vision, I ignored the feeble peripheral sputterings of my physical senses. I denied what my eyes could see, what my ears could hear. My friends, though, must have sensed the truth. Yet they willingly came back with me to this perilous place. Why? I can think of no other reason except selfless loyalty—and love.

"I'm seriously annoyed that Kenny isn't hurling a halibut against the window," remarked Petey.

"And where's Norris with a timely brick?" demanded Honky.

"It's my fault," I said. "I told Darla and Zeb not to wait. I said everything would be fine. It's all my fault."

"Well, we wanted to come back too," said Honky. "It wasn't just your decision, Robin. I do regret that I'll never be able to see Honky Junior take wing. I guess he's Julie's child after all."

"That's right," I said. "I was wrong about that too. Sure he's a pigeon, but so are we."

"Yes, but we're pretty exceptional pigeons," said Honky, nibbling on a stale millet seed.

"In light of the present circumstances," said Petey, "I'm re-evaluating my rejection of Blanche. Marriage to her now seems slightly preferable to dissection by Maryanne."

"You know what I regret the most?" I asked. "That Darla is going to wind up with that scoundrel Zeb. She deserves better."

"Well, Robin, she's always loved you," Honky pointed out.

"Yes, I see that now. Why was I so blind?"

"He is never so blind as the pigeon who will not see," remarked Honky.

"I still detest your dimestore homilies," said Petey.

"Damn," I said, "we've got to get out of this cage."

"Well you know, Robin," said Petey, "I used to give that notion some thought—purely as an engineering challenge. I'd mull the problem over while enjoying my Drag-O-Matic."

"It was *our* Drag-O-Matic," said Honky. "And what did you conclude?"

"I observed that the apparatus in question is an externally mounted double-latching lock. To open the door, one must click over the sliding bolt, then push down on the release lever. Access to both from inside is blocked by the large stainless steel shield. I eventually concluded escape was impossible."

"That's a big help," muttered Honky.

"There's a slight difference now," I pointed out.

"Is there?" asked Petey. "I'm not sure extreme desperation affects the calculations."

"We now have a tool," I said.

"What tool?" demanded Honky.

"Your leg."

CHAPTER 26

"Where's Maryanne now," I asked.

Honky looked around. "Still shoveling cat shit three aisles over. Hurry, Robin, I can't balance here forever on one foot."

"Don't worry," said Petey. "You don't have forever."

Gripping Honky's golden leg stub in my beak, I thrust it down toward the sliding bolt from above the metal shield. The rounded tip of shiny metal barely made contact with the spherical bolt handle. I applied lateral pressure. The bolt moved a few millimeters. I pushed again.

"Whatever you do, Robin, don't drop it," whispered Honky. "I won't have a leg to stand on."

I pushed again. The bolt slid almost to its release point, but now its handle was out of reach. I moved my gripping point precariously up the cap, and tried again. The tip just reached the handle, I pressed sideways, the bolt slid free. Then the door to the lab opened, I gave a start, and the glittering cap tumbled to the floor.

"Hey, Maryanne!" called a voice.

The vile traitoress looked up from a bank of cages. "Eldon! You're three hours early. This is unprecedented."

"Couldn't sleep," he said, hanging his grungy backpack on a hook beside the door and sauntering into the room. "I thought I'd relieve you early, since I know you have that big paper to write."

"How nice," she said. "I finally settled on a topic: Images of Castration Anxiety in the Sexism of Hammett's Alienated Anti-hero Sam Spade."

"Sounds like a real ball bruiser," he replied. "Glad I was a music major before I flunked out of the j.c."

"Tom and I want to come see your band, Eldon. What's its cute name?"

"The Sniveling Idiots. It's not cute, Maryanne. We got a gig at the Berkeley Grind. Friday at midnight."

"I think I'm off Friday. Maybe we'll come."

She's got a boyfriend, I thought. Big deal. The guy better watch his back when she's around.

"Cool," said Eldon. "Hey, I hear the Killer Pigeons showed up."

"Yes, Dr. Milbrene wants them processed tonight."

"Did you like do it already?" he asked.

"I did one," she replied, walking toward us. "The rest are over here."

"What did the test show?" asked Eldon, following her.

"Oh, the usual: enlarged liver from the alcohol, seriously occluded arteries from the rich diet, and, of course, advanced lung degeneration from the cigarettes."

"Our lifestyle!" exclaimed Honky. "It's hazardous to our health!"

"Yep, those are the Killer Pigeons all right," said Eldon, peering into our cage. "There's the white one, the fat one, and the red one. Hey, the white one's missing his little peg leg thing."

"Oh, he had it before," said Maryanne, looking about. "Here it is on the floor. He must have dropped it."

Maryanne pushed the precious peg through the bars of the cage; Honky immediately returned it to his stump.

"Say, whyn't you go on home, Maryanne?" said Eldon. "I can

process these dudes."

"You don't mind, Eldon?"

"Nah. That feisty red one used to bite me. As the song says, it's payback time."

I gulped. So much for Eldon's incessant drivel about peace and love.

"Thanks, Eldon," said Maryanne, putting on her coat. "They were kind of my favorites. I wasn't looking forward to . . . working on them."

"Don't you worry, babe," said Eldon. "They won't feel a thing."

"Good-bye, boys!" she called, picking up her purse.

"Good-bye, murderer!" we chirped.

She left. Eldon looked us over. His broad smile could only be described as diabolical.

"Yep," he sang. "Ol' Eldon got here just in the nick of time."

* * *

"The Beatles had Brian Epstein," said Eldon, leaning over until his inflamed nose nearly touched the wires of our cage. I couldn't decide which was worse: his pimples or his breath. "And the Sniveling Idiots have the Killer Pigeons."

"What's he talking about?" asked Honky.

"Maybe he wants us to manage his band," Petey suggested hopefully.

"Now, boys," Eldon continued, "I could take you in that room and process you dudes for $8.45 an hour. Or I can haul your little feathered asses over to the San Francisco cops and collect $10,000. Which would you do?"

"It's an ethical dilemma," agreed Petey.

"I know what you're thinking," said Eldon. "You're thinking what could ol' Eldon do with $10,000?"

"Get a haircut?" ventured Honky.

"Buy a toothbrush," suggested Petey.

"I'll tell you what I could do. I could get our CD produced. I can get the Sniveling Idiots on the road to subterranean notoriety."

"What the hell is that?" asked Honky.

"That's what young people of Eldon's generation strive for in place of success," I explained.

"And that's not all," he continued. "I can get a new amp for my bass. Who knows, I might even have enough left over for some of that joltin' Mendo Gold. And I owe it all to three little pigeons who came home to their papa."

"There's no need to be insulting," said Honky.

"Honky, get set to lend me your leg," said Petey. "If he comes any closer, I'll poke out his eye."

* * *

On the road to San Francisco. Where exactly I can't say, since Eldon covered our cage with some sort of funky blanket. From the cage's angle of inclination, the sounds of mechanical rumbling, and Eldon's nearby presence (revealed by his loud "singing"), I've deduced our cage has been placed beside him on the front seat of his car.

"What's that horrible song?" asked Honky, greedily inhaling Eldon's second-hand smoke.

"It sounds like a punk version of 'We're in the Money'," said Petey. "Hey, don't bogart the air."

"I'm not bogarting the air. I'm just breathing."

"OK, Honky," I said. "Let's have your leg again."

"Sure," he said, plucking it from his stump. "Only this time don't drop it."

"You shouldn't tell me that," I snapped. "It's hard enough doing the job under this kind of pressure. My nerves are shot!"

"Sorry, Robin," he replied. "Feel free to drop my leg. I've always wanted to see the inside of prison while hopping about on one foot."

As before, I clung to the wires of the cage and thrust the cap down toward the latching apparatus.

"Too bad Eldon pushed the bolt back," said Petey.

"I know," said Honky. "The guy is usually so reliably slipshod."

Concentrating intently, I struggled to slide back the locking bolt, while somehow retaining my grip on the pen cap despite the constant jolting of the moving car. At last I felt the bolt click free. I pulled the cap back into the cage and paused to quiet my racing heart.

"Good job, Robin," said Honky. "We're half-way there."

"What do we do if you get the door open?" asked Petey.

"Bail out a window," I replied.

"And if they're all rolled up?" said Honky.

"Go for Eldon. Big time."

Unfortunately, the loop of wire that formed the release lever presented a much smaller target than the fat handle of the bolt. And it was positioned tightly up against the metal door shield. Again and again I pressed down against it, only to have the tip of the cap slip off. Then Eldon paused in his song, the car slowed to a stop, and we felt a gust of fume-laden air. A moment later, the car accelerated and Eldon resumed his serenade to affluence.

"He probably paid the toll for the bridge," whispered Petey.

"Ask not for whom the bridge tolls," said Honky.

I resumed my efforts, this time experimenting by holding onto the clip and prying with the wider end of the cap. It worked! I felt the lever move away from the shield. Quickly, I turned the cap around, pressed the tip against the loop, pushed it down, and felt the door move on its hinges. I tossed Honky his peg and pushed. The door swung open an inch against the constricting blanket.

"OK, men," I said, "when I give the sign, we throw all of our weight against this door. One. Two. Three. *Go!*"

We shoved, the door moved, a gap appeared, I squeezed through, then Honky, then Petey. We struggled to find an opening in the enveloping folds of musty blanket.

"Hey, what the fuck!" we heard Eldon cry. We felt the car swerve, a hand pulled back the blanket. Daylight! We hit the floor and ducked under the front seat.

"Shit!" screamed Eldon.

The car swerved again. A hand groped desperately for us. Then two hands. The car lurched and skidded. Horns blared all around us. The car swerved, spun around violently, and rolled over. Again. And again. Metal shattered, glass exploded. A thud of impact. More skidding. More thuds. Then we were at rest and I saw light and felt a chill breeze.

"Men!" I shouted. "This way!"

"Actually," I heard Honky say, "I'm a pigeon."

CHAPTER 27

Petey insisted we stop for a quick breakfast on the Pigeon Chow Lady, then we flew on to the Palace of Fine Arts.

"Honky, you're back!" exclaimed Julie, overjoyed to see us. "And Robin too!"

"Even Petey!" sang Blanche.

"Where's Darla?" I asked urgently.

"She's off with Zeb," replied Julie.

"Doing what?" I demanded.

"Gathering nest materials," replied Blanche. "An activity I expect we'll be engaged in shortly," she added, gazing severely at Petey.

I was too late! A black despair seized my heart. "Miss Gerigar," I said, "There's something I must know. Do pigeons mate for life?"

Verna looked up thoughtfully from her nest. "Well, that is a matter of some conjecture. Now, you take the case of . . ."

"Of course, pigeons mate for life," interjected Darla, fluttering down from the concrete ledge. Scraps of shredded paper were clutched in her lovely knobby toes.

"I was afraid of that," I said despairingly. "You were right, Darla. Maryanne revealed herself to be a ruthless murderer."

"Oh, that's terrible!" she exclaimed. "What happened?"

"Where's Yancy?" demanded Phoebe, emerging from her trailer

doorway.

"Uh, actually, that's how Maryanne qualifies as a murderer," Petey explained.

"He's . . . dead?" she asked, stricken.

"The guy was a hero," Honky lied consolingly. "He gave his life for science."

"I'm cursed!" she wailed, retreating into her mobile home.

"I've got more bad news," I announced. "We're pigeons."

"Speak for yourself," sniffed Sunny.

"Being a pigeon is nothing to be ashamed of," said Sister Angelina charitably.

"It certainly isn't," agreed Miss Gerigar. "Congratulations, Robin, on your successful identity integration. It's a momentous step toward positive mental health."

"Of course, we're pigeons," laughed Darla.

"It's very nice being a pigeon," added Wally Junior from the trailer. "Except they don't make Ferraris in our size."

"You mean, Darla, you knew you were a pigeon?" I asked.

"Well, Robin, I did experience some initial confusion. I identified strongly with my human caretakers. And Dr. Milbrene always referred to us as test animals or ladies and men. I think now the evil man was being facetious. But a girl knows in her heart what she is. Besides, people can't fly."

"No, they can't," I agreed. It all seemed so logical now.

"Not to be superior about it," said Julie, "but I feel our ability to fly and scavenge for food and live together in a crowded city under often difficult circumstances makes our species rather special. It's, it's beautiful being a pigeon."

"You're very beautiful," said Honky.

"Oh, Honky!"

Darla smiled and gazed expectantly at me.

I felt another wave of despair. "Well, Darla, I guess I should congratulate you. I hope you and Zeb will be very happy together."

"That's not very likely, Robin," she said softly.

"Why not?"

"Pigeons mate for life."

First confusion, then a faint glimmer of hope.

"You mean . . ."

"That's right, my dearest."

"Oh, Darla!"

"Oh, Robin!"

Blanche smiled and gazed expectantly at Petey.

"Damn," he said, rubbing his side, "I think I bruised my gizzard in that rollover."

* * *

"I'm sorry I let you down, Robin," said Kenny, returning that afternoon from a visit with his mother. "I wanted to go see how you were doing in Berkeley, but Zeb said you would be mad if we showed up."

"You didn't let us down, Kenny," I replied. "By the way, where is Zeb?"

"He and Jasper are out on a major bender," reported Norris. "The beer keg has been refilled."

"That's intriguing news," said Petey.

"Petey, think of your liver," I reminded him.

"I can't, Robin. All of my available brain capacity is devoted to fixating on the cigarette I'm madly denying myself."

"Then think about our press coverage. Honky, what does Kenny's newspaper say?"

"Uh, the headline is: Escaping KPs Cause Massive Commute Tie-up."

"We've achieved true fame," said Petey. "They're now referring to us by our initials."

"Honky, what's it say about Eldon?" I asked.

"It says he's in San Francisco General Hospital with moderate injuries. They're hailing him as a hero. The mayor was photographed at his bedside autographing his casts. And big-time record producers are phoning with audition offers for the Sniveling Idiots."

"This could be his big break," I said.

"You mean his third big break," said Honky. "The first two were compound fractures to his arm and leg."

"Any more about us?" asked Petey.

"There's a quote from Dr. Milbrene. He's denying any knowledge of our return to his lab."

"What a liar," I said.

"Actually, the big news is the Fubsy Bug invasion," continued Honky. "It says here tourism is down eighty percent. The bugs are giving the visitors the creeps—chasing them away in droves. Conventions are being canceled and the hotels are virtually empty. Restaurants are suffering too."

"I thought the dumpster pickings have been pretty slim lately," said Darla. "Fortunately, we've had the Fubsy Bugs to fall back on."

"You mean you eat them too?" I asked.

"Of course, Robin. They're quite tasty. And nourishing too. Honky Junior is growing by leaps and bounds."

"I noticed," I replied. No longer pink and downy, Honky's stepson had reached the prickly, ungainly stage. Too bad the beauty of the pigeon does not extend to the squab.

"Here," she said, offering me a bug. "Care to try one?"

I grasped the squirming, furry thing in my beak, fought against revulsion, and gulped. No rising gorge, no waves of nausea. In fact, it wasn't bad. Not bad at all. Lingering on the palate were flavors of smoked venison, spicy rosemary, and an earthy hint of wild chanterelles.

"It's delicious," I said.

"I know," said Darla. "I just wish everyone would try them."

"Darla darling," I said, "you've just given me an idea."

* * *

We went to Union Square. We went to Civic Center. We went to the Transbay Terminal. We went to Fisherman's Wharf and Pier 39. Everywhere we went, we called together our fellow pigeons, and invited them to sample Fubsy Bugs. Impressed, they told their friends, who told their friends. When we had covered the city, we went to Brisbane, San Mateo, and the peaceful cemeteries of Colma. We flew on to the East Bay. And Marin County. Even down to Silicon Valley and San Jose. Soon the skies over San Francisco were black with millions of hungry, civic-minded pigeons. Vast flocks descended on the parks and the back yards, the Marina Green and the slopes of Twin Peaks, the beaches and the Castro district, even the manicured lawns of Seacliff. Everywhere our fellow pigeons landed they eagerly devoured Fubsy Bugs.

At my side throughout this endeavor, laboring harder than anyone, was Darla.

"It's a curious thing," I said to her one day while clearing out a large FB population in Washington Park. "Since I've been eating Fubsy Bugs, I've lost my taste for cigarettes."

"I'm happy to hear it, Robin dear. And you seem much stronger."

"You know, I can't believe people actually smoke those things."

"Kenny's given them up too, darling. Zeb still smokes, poor thing. Of course, his character is regrettably weak."

"I thought you liked him, Darla."

"I rather enjoyed his attentions for a time, Robin. But I could never love someone who is deceitful and steals food from small children. I had a talk with him yesterday. He's decided to move in with Phoebe."

"Really? I didn't think he liked her."

"Norris helped him decide."

"Ah, yes. That falcon can be very persuasive."

Suddenly day turned to night as thousands of pigeons stampeded into the sky.

I turned and waved to Norris and Angelina, who had arrived to perform the ceremonial "Blessing of the Fubsy Feast."

"Robin dear, this blessing business isn't really helping," said Darla. "They're terrifying our workers. It's putting us days behind schedule."

"I know, Darla, but what can I do? It was Sister Angelina's idea, and I don't want to hurt her feelings."

"Robin, would you say that we are preying upon these Fubsy Bugs?"

"Well, I suppose you could put it that way, Darla—if you considered it from the bugs' point of view. Not that I do."

"Therefore, you'd agree that one can prey without being particularly religious?"

"Darla darling, what are you saying?"

"Robin, I don't think Angelina is a nun."

"Really? But she seems so devout."

"Yes, well, sometimes a girl makes accommodations in the interests of love. One pretends to enthusiasms one may not share. Don't look so worried, Robin, I do enjoying picnicking on Fubsy Bugs with you. I just thought perhaps you could have a chat with Norris."

"I'll do that," I said. "He might be interested to hear she's not a nun. Very interested indeed."

* * *

The day after we gave Mrs. M's severe Fubsy Bug infestation our personal attention, she called a press conference in her decimated but now pristine garden. At her side were the Pigeon Chow Lady, Effie Perine, and other prominent citizens. Mrs. M pointed out that they had received reports from all parts of the city of Killer Pigeons waging a heroic campaign against the demon bugs.

"We ought to call them—not Killer Pigeons—but Rescue Pigeons," she declared. "They are rescuing this city from financial ruin."

Then Mrs. M dropped a bombshell. She divulged that a high city official had informed her privately that the incriminating body parts found in the tree were fake.

"These birds are not killers," thundered the Pigeon Chow Lady. "They're heroes!"

"And excellent dancers too," added Effie.

Two hours later the mayor called his own press conference to announce that all charges had been dropped. "I'm not sure what attacked me that night," he explained. "It might have been bats." He also announced that the Board of Supervisors had just passed emergency legislation making it a misdemeanor to interfere with the activities of Rescue Pigeons. Violators would be subject to arrest and fines of $10,000.

The newspapers took up the campaign. Everywhere in the city, people came out of their homes to hail and praise passing pigeons. Rich snacks were offered up, until it was observed that this commendable but misguided generosity was hindering the all-important anti-Fubsy Bug campaign.

There were other consequences. Popular opinion turned against Eldon. In the editorial pages, our abductor was denounced as a "long-haired opportunist" and "heavy metal profiteer." The Sniveling Idiots were bounced by their new record company. Curiously, this made the band even more popular with their small coterie of rabid fans, thus earning our former lab attendant a small measure of subterranean notoriety.

* * *

After the last known Fubsy Bug in the city had been plucked off a German tourist on Nob Hill, we bid farewell to the doleful stone ladies (they seemed sad to see us go), and moved back to our lavishly refurbished Gold Rush Sherry sign. Nests soon appeared in many chambers, including the spacious view apartment I share with Darla. Putting religious issues aside, Norris and

Angelina jointly vowed to forsake celibacy. Kenny met a lovely seagull, Nicole, who is working on overcoming her irrational prejudice against pigeons. Sunny continues abrasively virile, but is receiving in-nest counseling from his mate. They think their new baby may be a female.

Wally Junior and Ina (no longer a baby) finally left their trailer home, but often drop by. The latter continues to snub Jasper's romantic overtures, not being attracted to older pigeons who smoke and twitch. Phoebe is worried about Zeb, who caught her moult germs and has developed a nasty cough to boot. He and Jasper are frequent visitors to the special pigeon window recently opened at the Top of the Mark by the grateful hotel management. All the sherry you can drink, and the fried pork rinds are always crisp. Plenty of smokes too, if you wish to ruin your health. We hardly go there ourselves.

* * *

"Have you heard the latest rumor?" I asked, lounging on top of our sign in the warm spring sunshine. "The rumor is Sam Spade is actually a pigeon."

"Who's spreading that nutty rumor?" asked Petey, dining on a cold stepped-on chicken nugget.

"Well, I am," I replied. "All the clues fit. That's why he wasn't really in love with Brigid."

"Then who was the guy in the alley?" asked Petey.

"Who knows," I replied. "It could have been anyone. It was very dark."

"OK, it makes a certain amount of sense," said Honky. "Petey, are you going to bogart that snack?"

"I am, yes. It's the only vice Blanche hasn't harangued out of me. Where have you been, anyway?"

"Working," said Honky. "You should try it sometime. I was helping Julie collect leaves for the FBs."

We are keeping a colony of Fubsy Bugs in reserve for snacks, infant food, and as a hedge against any possible revival in the city of anti-pigeon sentiment. My sweet Darla thinks of everything.

"I've been thinking," I said.

"Uh-oh," said Honky.

"Things have been pretty calm around here."

"Too calm," said Petey. "What's on your mind, Robin?"

"Ted Trinello."

"But Ted's in jail," said Honky. "After recovering from a near-fatal case of cat-scratch fever, he's now facing 17 felony counts. You're not . . ."

"That's right, men," I said, lowering my voice. "We spring brave Ted. It's the least we can do. Now, here's my plan . . ."

C.D. Payne was born in 1949 in Akron, Ohio, the former "Rubber Capital of the World" famed for its tire factories. He shares a birthday with P.T. Barnum, a fact which has influenced his life profoundly. After graduating from Harvard College in 1971, he moved to California, where he's worked as a newspaper editor, graphic artist, cartoonist, typesetter, photographer, proofreader, carpenter, trailer park handyman, and advertising copywriter. He is married and lives in Sonoma County, north of San Francisco.